Low-Fat
Mexican Cooking

Patrick Earvolino
Illustrations by Lisa Kirkpatrick

Voyageur Press

A Jennifer, por enseñarme a soñar

Edited by Michael Dregni
Designed by Leslie Ross

Printed in the United States of America

96   97   98   99   00   5   4   3   2   1

Library of Congress Cataloging-in-Publication Data
Earvolino, Patrick J., 1968–
    Low-fat Mexican cooking / by Patrick J. Earvolino.
        p.   cm.
    Includes index.
    ISBN 0-89658-277-9
    1. Cookery, Mexican.   2. Low-fat diet—Recipes.   I. Title.
TX716.M4E27   1996
641.5'638—dc20   95-40342
                                                                    CIP

Distributed in Canada by Raincoast Books, 8680 Cambie Street, Vancouver, B.C. V6P 6M9

Published by Voyageur Press, Inc.
123 North Second Street, P.O. Box 338, Stillwater, MN 55082 U.S.A.
612-430-2210, fax 612-430-2211

Please write or call, or stop by, for our free catalog of natural history publications. Our toll-free number to place an order or to obtain a free catalog is 800-888-WOLF (800-888-9653).

Educators, fundraisers, premium and gift buyers, publicists, and marketing managers: Looking for creative products and new sales ideas? Voyageur Press books are available at special discounts when purchased in quantities, and special editions can be created to your specifications. For details contact the marketing department.

Acknowledgments
Muchas Gracias

It is my fortune to have the opportunity to express my deepest gratitude to the many wonderful people who helped me achieve this dream. First and foremost, I would like to thank Jennifer Scoville and Carl Bacher for their aid in cooking, testing, and verifying recipes, as well as keeping the project afloat throughout the last two-and-a-half years. Many thanks also to Marcia Snell, for giving Jenni and me the opportunity of a lifetime; Kelly Yelmene, for her kindness, generosity, and friendship; and Juan Carlos Salcido Roland, for putting us up and putting up with us in Fortín de las Flores. A big gracias as well to the kind folks at the Guild House in Cuernavaca.

I would also like to thank Danny and Jackie Potts, as well as Nick Barbaro and Susan Moffat, for sheltering us after returning—homeless, carless, and jobless—from abroad; and Tivoli Majors and Whitney Temple, who selflessly let me hog their computers for months on end until I could buy my own. I am also indebted to María Delgado, whose advice and friendship helped me through some of the most difficult stretches of this undertaking; Harold Eggers, for all his advice; Dave Cook, who inspired me by example to keep typing; and Beth Miller and her golden palate. Thank you also, Lisa Kirkpatrick, for the splendid artwork; Jeffrey Grier and Al Kineer for culinary counsel; Gerald McLeod, for loaning me a long-overdue cookbook; and Douglas Garner, for motivating me to write a book. Y muchas gracias al Insituto Colectivo de Lengua y Cultura Cuauhnahuac, especialmente a Bertha Flores Manzano, una gran cocinera, y a todas las otras cocineras mexicanas que me ensearon la comida y la cultura mexicana.

Finally, I would like to thank the following people for their general support and understanding over the course of this endeavor: my family, Gerald Corder, Amanda McManus, Sam and Deborah Wilson, Virginia Wood, and Scott Snell.

Patrick Earvolino

❧ Contents

Chapter 6: *Platos al Lado*/Side Dishes *131*

Chapter 7: *Sopas*/Soups   159

Chapter 8: *Botanas*/Snacks   179

Introduction
The Wholesome Enchilada

I noticed some interesting statistics in the news recently. Not only does salsa now outsell ketchup in the United States, but more Americans are now eating at Mexican restaurants than at Italian eateries. Mexican food has become America's favorite ethnic cuisine.

At the time of this revelation, I was living in Austin, Texas, where these statistics hardly raised an eyebrow. Texas is home to a wealth of traditional Mexican and American-Mexican restaurants. But as a recently relocated Yankee just beginning to explore Mexican food, I was surprised to learn that my growing obsession was part of such a momentous transition.

The American diet has been moving in another direction as well. Most nutritionists today tell us to limit our diet to 2,000–2,500 calories a day and our fat consumption to 60–65 grams a day, with a maximum of 30 percent of total calories coming from fat. Unfortunately, these guidelines are difficult—if not impossible—to follow inside the doors of a typical American-Mexican restaurant. In fact, when the Center for Science in the Public Interest (CSPI), a Washington, D.C.–based consumers' interest group, published the results of its 1994 investigation into the nutritional value of Mexican food in the United States, virtually the entire cuisine was panned. For example, the CSPI's study concluded that eating a plate of *chiles rellenos* (stuffed peppers) was equivalent to consuming a whole stick of butter.

Personally, I did not need this report to alert me to the bodily detriment of Mexican food. When I moved to Austin in 1990, I ate enchiladas three times a week, gained ten pounds, and suffered my first attack of heartburn. I knew I needed to curb my habit before it got out of hand, yet I was unabashedly addicted to Mexican food.

I spent the next few years developing low-fat TexMex cooking techniques and cutting down on fatty ingredients such as cheese, sour cream, guacamole, and cooking oil. The positive results plus my continued fascination with Mexican cooking promptly inspired a trip to the horse's mouth.

From September 1993 to June 1994, I traveled throughout Mexico, sampling dishes, collecting recipes, and researching a healthy translation of our neighbors' exquisite but heavy fare. In cities such as Oaxaca, Tepotzlán, Fortín de las Flores, Mexico City, San Cristóbal de Las Casas, Mérida, and Zihuatanejo, I frequented the popular restaurants, the unpretentious *fondas* (luncheonettes), the mind-boggling markets, and the splendid street carts. I took cooking classes in Cuernavaca from chef and restaurant owner Bertha Flores Manzano and observed the kitchens of many friends' *muchachas*, or family maids, whose friendliness and culinary expertise remain an inspiration.

After returning to the United States, I translated the recipes I had gathered and set out to create a low-fat Mexican cuisine compatible with the advice of the United States' nutritional counselors. In developing these low-fat dishes, I established several main objectives:

To retain authentic Mexican flavors. This is something many Mexican cookbooks in the United States have no regard for, substituting or adding inappropriate spices, herbs, and other ingredients.

To meet fat requirements of the recommended American diet. Per serving, entrées average 8 grams of fat (360 calories); side dishes, 2.5 grams (150 calories); soups, 3 grams (160 calories); breakfasts, 8.5 grams (380 calories); and snacks, 4 grams (250 calories). In almost all of these dishes, 30 percent or fewer of the calories come from fat; the others are only slightly over this mark.

To keep it simple and cheap. After learning a few basic techniques, you will find most dishes are inexpensive and easy to prepare. All ingredients can be found at well-stocked supermarkets or Hispanic markets.

To provide a glimpse of Mexican culture. There is a remarkable reverence for food in Mexico, and exploring the cuisine is a great way to get to know the character of the country—some of which I hope is conveyed by the anecdotes accompanying the recipes.

Many people in the United States are excited about sampling a greater variety of Mexican food or simply wish to continue to eat what Mexican dishes they like without suffering negative nutritional consequences. It is for these folks that I have written this book. In the following pages, you will discover the tongue-tingling celebration of life that is Mexican cuisine without unwanted fats and oils to ruin the party.

∾ What is Mexican Food?

When I was growing up in Massachusetts, "Mexican Night" meant a dinner of prefab corn shells filled with ground beef, cheese, and a mysterious powdered seasoning. What these taco-kit creations lacked in flavor they made up for in fat, and the token lettuce and tomato toppings did little to improve them. I grew to dread these packets of grease and chili powder, and for a long time I avoided anything labeled "Mexican food."

Then I moved to the Lone Star State. For those rusty on its history, Texas was actually part of Coahuila, Mexico, until just 160 years ago. The result of this historical tie is a legacy of Mexican culture that permeates Planet Texas, reflected prominently in the famous cuisine known as TexMex. The staples of Texas life—nachos, burritos, *fajitas, chile con queso,* soft flour tacos—were a revelation to my taste buds.

I started to explore TexMex cookery. I discovered that it was just one—albeit the most popular—of several distinct types of Mexican cooking in Texas. Others included Interior Mexican, Coastal Mexican, Southwestern (United States) Mexican, and CalMex. I spent time in Mexico. I sampled Pueblan, Oaxacan, Yucatecan, Jaliscan, Chiapan, and more regional varieties of traditional Mexican cuisine. The negative association of Mexican Night slid into the forgettable past, replaced by a single persistent question: What, exactly, is Mexican food?

To answer this question, it is helpful to imagine the diet of Mexicans in the days before Christopher Columbus and the Spanish conquistadors. Just as it is today, Mexican food at that time was centered around the "Big Three" ingredients: corn, chiles, and beans. A few other New World products, such as tomatoes, tomatillos, squash, avocados, and nuts, formed a colorful supporting cast, and by roasting, boiling, and steaming these essentials, Mexicans were adept at creating exquisite food out of practically nothing. Significantly, this peasant cuisine was truly low in fat; no vegetable oil or lard was used in cooking.

The Conquest brought a plethora of Old World ingredients to Mexico, many of which were quickly incorporated into the cuisine. Chicken, pork, spices, olive oil, garlic, wheat, oregano, parsley, and other spices were all used to enhance existing dishes and devise wonderful new ones. Rice was brought from the Far East. Mexican cooks started using animal fat and vegetable oil, ironically converting their light fare into a high-fat smorgasbord. They learned how to make cheese. Tamales were softened by using lard. *Mole poblano,* a chile-chocolate-nut sauce that has become the unofficial national dish, was invented in a Pueblan monastery. *El mestizaje*—the mixing of indigenous and Spanish cultures—was born.

Over the last few hundred years, cooking south of the border has changed with the times while remaining characteristically Mexican. Cooks still make their tortillas from scratch, but many have acquiesced to using *presadores* (tortilla presses) to pat them out. Many dishes are still prepared on a *comal,* a large metal sheet heated over an open fire, while others are now cooked atop stoves in cast-iron skillets and clay or metal pots. Blenders are often standard equipment, and even though new dishes are constantly being created, the Big Three remain at the center of the Mexican diet.

One of the difficulties in further defining Mexican food lies in its decidedly regional nature. The dishes of Texas and northern Mexico feature lots of beef, cheese, Anaheim peppers, flour tortillas, and pinto beans, whereas the food of south-central Mexico emphasizes chicken, pork, *chiles poblanos,* corn tortillas, and black beans. On the other hand, the seafood dishes prepared along the many miles of Mexican coastline are largely dissimilar to either of these interior cuisines, and the turkey, *chile habanero,* and other staples of the Yucatán are so exotic to most Mexicans that the peninsula is considered practically another culinary country.

At the same time, many intra- and international dishes are familiar to most Mexicans and non-Mexicans alike. *Chiles rellenos,* enchiladas, tacos, *quesadillas, sopa de tortilla,* and so on can all be found pretty much anywhere in Mexico, in Texas, and even beyond.

It would be a shame to limit a definition of Mexican cuisine to these dishes. In an analogy to Italian cuisine, these items are the Mexican equivalents of pizza, spaghetti, and lasagna. To obtain a true sense of Mexican food, the counterparts of pesto, calamari, and gnocchi must be included. Only then will one begin to taste the incomparable cuisine of Mexico, the kitchen of the New World.

¡Buen provecho!

The Nutritional Analysis and Testing Recipes

The nutritional analyses of the recipes in this book were performed using the Key Home Gourmet software by Softkey. The database of nutritional information used in the analyses was assembled from U.S. Department of Agriculture (USDA) research publications and information from food manufacturers.

I and my fellow Mexican travel mates and cooks, Carl Bacher and Jennifer L. Scoville, kitchen-tested each recipe in this book to assure its quality, authenticity, and yield. Yields are based on an average meal of one entrée plus one soup and one or two side dishes, accompanied by two warm corn tortillas and a salsa per person.

Chapter 1

The Basics of
Low-Fat Mexican Cooking

It does not take special tools, impossible-to-find ingredients, or complicated techniques to prepare low-fat Mexican food. What is required is an open mind. Novice cook or expert, one should forget the dogma of European cuisine and greasy classic Mexican cookery and discover the soul of healthy Mexican cooking through the basic principles, techniques, and ingredients described in this chapter.

The naturally fatty ingredients of Mexican cuisine are beef, pork, eggs, nuts, cheese, avocado, cream, lard, and oil. Although this list seems long, the items on it are used less than you might think in preparing most Mexican dishes, particularly those of central and southern Mexico, where most of the people live. The ingredients that form the bulk of Mexican food are light meats, such as chicken, turkey, and seafood; grains and legumes, including rice, wheat, and beans; and fruits and vegetables, such as corn, chiles, tomatoes, tomatillos, squash, and tropical fruits. These healthy raw ingredients would satisfy the guidelines of the USDA Food Pyramid quite nicely if they did not tend to be heavily processed with lard and oil before reaching the dinner table. Thus, the spirit of low-fat Mexican cooking lies in preparing basic, healthy ingredients in ways that avoid or diminish the use of lard and oil without sacrificing flavor.

⌇ Cooking Techniques

Some low-fat Mexican cooking techniques are novel, many are familiar, but none are particularly complicated. By reading through the following simple processes and familiarizing yourself with them, you will be prepared to make any of the recipes in this book.

Sautéing Onion and Garlic

When cooking Mexican food, onion and garlic are almost never sautéed until brown. Simply sauté them in a small amount of corn oil until the onion is soft and translucent but not brown.

Seasoning Oil

A common method of flavoring many Mexican sauces is to cook them in oil seasoned with onion. Place a slice of white onion in a frying pan with the oil to be seasoned and heat over medium heat until the onion is blackened. Discard the onion. The oil is seasoned and ready for use.

Toasting and Grinding Herbs and Spices

In general, spices and herbs, such as cumin seed, oregano leaf, clove, and marjoram, should be toasted in a hot skillet until fragrant, then ground in a spice grinder or a mortar before use.

Blending

It may sound silly, but there are different degrees of blending depending on the desired consistency of the product. If a smooth, uniform sauce is called for, then high-speed, long-term blending is OK and will be indicated by the phrase "blend until smooth" or "purée."

When a textured chunky sauce is required, as for the majority of table salsas, the blending should consist of short, low-speed, "chop" pulses, as indicated by "coarse blending" or "pulse blending." When performing this type of blending, check the contents of the blender until the desired consistency is attained and avoid creating air bubbles in the sauce.

Broiling and Seeding Tomatoes

Two important methods of preparing tomatoes are broiling and seeding. To broil tomatoes, place them 4–6 inches (10–15 cm) from the broiler flame on a shallow pan lined with aluminum foil. Cook them 5–8 minutes (5 minutes for small tomatoes, 8 for large), then turn them over and cook another 5–8 minutes. Remove only the hardened parts of their skins, leaving the rest on for flavor, or remove all the skin if the recipe calls for broiled and peeled tomatoes. To seed tomatoes, simply halve them and squeeze out the seeds.

Poaching and Shredding Chicken Breast

Poached shredded chicken breast is a common ingredient of Mexican food that is especially prominent in light Mexican cuisine. To poach one or several split chicken breasts, put them in a large saucepan or pot, cover with water, and add 1–3 crushed garlic cloves, a thick slice of white onion, a few peppercorns (optional), and a pinch salt. Cover the pan and gently simmer the contents for 25 minutes. Allow the chicken to cool in the water, then remove it. Remove and discard the skin, shred the meat, and discard the bones or save them for making soup stock. One large split breast yields $1\frac{1}{2}$–2 cups (375–500 ml) of shredded meat.

Roasting and Peeling Fresh Chiles

Roasting is a favored way of preparing fresh chiles in Mexican cooking. To roast *chiles poblanos* or Anaheim peppers, heat them directly over an open flame by laying them on the burner grill and turning them with tongs or by impaling them near the stem on a long fork and turning them over the flame. To roast *chiles serranos* or *jalapeños,* heat them in a dry nonstick or cast-iron skillet over medium-high heat. (For those with an electric range, this method can be used to roast *chiles poblanos* or Anaheim peppers as well.)

In either case, heat the chiles until their skins are evenly charred and begin to blister (2–4 minutes, being extremely careful not to overcook the flesh of the chiles), then remove them from the heat, seal them in a plastic bag, and let them "sweat" for 10 minutes. Remove the chiles and peel their skins—the flesh should be green, not brown, and cooked, but firm.

A convenient alternative roasting method is to place fresh chiles of any type under the broiler, about 2 inches (5 cm) from the flame, and turn them periodically until their skins are evenly charred. With this method, it is extremely important to avoid overcooking the flesh of the chiles, particularly the large chiles to be used for stuffing. Remove the chiles, sweat them, and remove their skins, as above. Always roast a few more chiles than the recipe calls for, as a few are usually unusable.

Toasting and Soaking Dried Chiles

In preparing Mexican food, dried chiles are often cleaned, then toasted and/or soaked before further use. To clean dried chiles, wipe off any dirt with a damp towel and remove and discard the stems.

Slit the chiles down one side, remove the heat-containing seeds and stringy veins, and spread the chile bodies out into single, flat pieces.

Toast these pieces by laying them in a dry skillet and heating them over medium heat, pressing occasionally with a spatula for even toasting. Heat them until they are darkened and fragrant, about 5 minutes per side. Be careful not to blister or burn the skin, as this will give the chiles a bitter taste.

Soak toasted or untoasted chiles by placing them in a bowl and covering them with a minimum of 1–1 ½ cups (250–375 ml) of boiling water for 10 minutes.

Warming Corn Tortillas

Mexican meals are nearly always served with warm corn or flour tortillas on the side. There are several simple ways to soften and warm these standard accompaniments. (Note that these methods differ from those used to soften tortillas for rolling enchiladas, which are discussed in the Enchiladas section of the "Gringo Grub" chapter.)

To warm corn tortillas, heat a cast-iron or nonstick frying pan over medium heat. Sprinkle a little water on each side of the tortilla, then lay it on the hot pan and heat the tortilla for 15–20 seconds without disturbing it. Flip the tortilla and heat for 15–20 seconds more. Repeat this process for as many tortillas as desired. Alternatively, place a stack of five to ten tortillas inside a zipper-lock plastic bag, seal, and heat in a microwave on high for 45–60 seconds (the time will vary depending on the microwave). For a single tortilla, heat in a plastic bag for 15–30 seconds in the microwave.

Warming Flour Tortillas

To warm flour tortillas, heat a cast-iron or nonstick frying pan over medium heat. Do not sprinkle water on the tortilla, as a flour tortilla contains a sufficient amount of moisture to heat as is. Lay the tortilla on the hot pan and heat the tortilla for 15–20 seconds without disturbing it. Flip the tortilla and heat for 15–20 seconds more. Repeat this process for as many tortillas as desired. Alternatively, place a stack of three to five tortillas inside a zipper-lock plastic bag, do not seal, and heat in a microwave on high for 30–45 seconds. For a single tortilla, heat in the microwave for 15–20 seconds.

Both corn and flour tortillas should be warmed immediately before serving. To keep them warm and soft throughout the meal, leave them in the plastic bag they were heated in, and wrap them in a dry dishtowel, or put them in a tortilla warmer immediately after heating.

༖ Common Ingredients of Low-Fat Mexican Cooking

Many of the ingredients used in this book are well known in the United States; others are not so familiar yet possible to find once you know what you're looking for. Listed here are some of the basic ingredients of low-fat Mexican cooking, followed by general information and uses for each. Mexican-Spanish names, availability, and possible substitutes are given where appropriate.

Allspice (*pimienta gorda*): Aromatic spice used in many dishes of Puebla, Oaxaca, and Veracruz to season *moles,* soups, stews, and beans.

Bay leaf (*hoja de laurel*): Dried leaf of the laurel tree used in pickled dishes called *escabeches* and used to season soups, sauces, and stews. Whole bay leaves should always be removed before serving if there is any danger of them being eaten.

Beans (*frijoles*): One of the Big Three ingredients of Mexican cuisine along with corn and chile. Pinto beans (*frijoles pintos*) are generally more popular in the north of Mexico; black beans (*frijoles negros*), in the south.

Cactus (*nopal*): Used in salads and soups. Chopped pieces of cactus, called *nopalitos,* are available packaged and ready to use in many supermarkets and Mexican food markets.

Cheese (*queso*): Reduced-fat cheddar and mozzarella cheeses are used as light substitutes, respectively, for two of Mexico's best known cheeses, *queso manchego* and *queso oaxaca*. Parmesan is used in place of the similar *queso añejo,* and a mild feta can be used as a substitute for *queso ranchero* (also known as *queso fresco*), an extremely popular farmer's cheese often crumbled over enchiladas and other dishes.

Chicken (*pollo*): Commonly poached, shredded, and combined with tortillas, chicken is the basis of countless entrees as well as Mexico's standard soup stock, *caldo de pollo*.

Chile peppers (*chiles*): See "Chiles and Mexican Cooking" following this section.

Chocolate (*chocolate*): Mexican chocolate is full of cinnamon and almond and contains surprisingly little fat. It usually comes in five or six 2-oz (56-g) wedges, individually wrapped inside a hexagonal package.

Chorizo: Sausage seasoned with chiles and spices, often crumbled and browned to be eaten with rice, eggs, in tacos, and so on.

Cilantro: One of the staple herbs of Mexican cooking, usually found in the fresh herb section of the supermarket. Also known as coriander or Chinese parsley, its broad, serrated leaves and tender upper stems are chopped *roughly* and used to season dishes or as an aromatic garnish for soups, tacos, and more. There is no substitute for fresh cilantro. Clip stems and store in 1 inch of water in an uncovered container; a bunch will last 7–10 days in the refrigerator.

Cinnamon (*canela*): Used in many sauces of southeastern Mexico and the essential ingredient of *cafe de olla,* or Mexican coffee, and the famous *mole poblano.*

Clove (*clavo*): Pungent spice sparingly used in many sauces and stews.

Corn (*elote,* meaning the "fruit" of the corn; *maíz,* meaning the corn plant): One of the Big Three ingredients of Mexican cuisine, along with chiles and beans, and the basis of the corn tortilla—the bread of Mexican food.

Corn flour (*masa harina*): Finely ground processed corn. Mixed with water, *masa harina* forms the basic tortilla dough, *masa*. This corn flour is not to be confused with cornmeal.

Cumin (*comino*): Used throughout Mexican cooking, usually in the form of ground seeds, not powder.

Egg substitute: Recommended brands include Better'n Eggs and Egg Beaters.

Epazote: Singular leafy herb definitive of Mexican cuisine. The jutting, serrated leaves are often stuffed in tamales or *quesadillas* and invariably added to a pot of black beans to impart an addictive, albeit acquired, taste. Seedlings are available at many nurseries, often labeled as wormseed, Mexican tea, or goosefoot. *Epazote* can be identified by its almost graphite-like odor. Although not similar, cilantro is usually an acceptable alternative.

Fruit (*fruta*): Mexico is home to a bounty of fruits. Some of the more popular are papaya, mango, guava (*guayaba*), banana (*plátano*), strawberry (*fresa*), cantaloupe (*melón*), watermelon (*sandía*), pineapple (*piña*), coconut (*coco*), orange (*naranja*), and grapefruit (*toronja*).

Garlic (*ajo*): Used extensively but moderately in Mexican salsas, soups, and sauces.

Jícama: Resembling a large contorted turnip, this interesting tuber has a tough, brown skin and sweet, white flesh. Its consistency is like that of a water chestnut and it is often peeled, chopped, and eaten as a salad with citrus, dried chile, and/or cilantro. It can be found in the produce section of many supermarkets. There is no substitute for jícama.

Lime (*limón*): Served with seafood, nuts, soups, vegetables, fruits, beer, and so on, a wedge of lime may be the most common garnish in Mexico. If possible, buy the small key limes instead of the big Persian ones.

Masa: Simple dough of processed corn flour and water used to make tortillas, tamales, and other Mexican carbohydrate staples.

Mushrooms (*hongos*): Button mushrooms are used in a variety of Mexican dishes, especially soups, enchiladas, *quesadillas,* and eggs or served as a seasoned side dish.

Oil (*aceite*): Common cooking oils are corn, olive, safflower, and vegetable.

Onion (*cebolla*): With few exceptions, use only white onion when cooking Mexican food.

Oregano (*oregano*): Used frequently in Mexican sauces, soups, and stews, and a main ingredient of pickled dishes known as *escabeches.*

Parsley (*perejil*): Popular ingredient of many soups and sauces. Use flat-leaf, Italian-style only.

Red snapper (*huachinango*): This Gulf native is possibly the most popular fish used in Mexican cuisine.

Rice (*arroz*): Mexican rice dishes are often cooked in a tomato or chicken broth base. In general, use long-grain white rice.

Shellfish (*mariscos):* With thousands of miles of coast, Mexico is a shellfish lover's paradise. Shrimp (*camarones*), octopus (*pulpo*), squid (*calamare*), oysters (*ostiones*), conch (*concha*), and snails (*caracoles*) abound.

Tortilla: The bread of Mexican food; see the chapter "*La Tortilla de Maíz.*"

Tomatillo (*tomate* or *tomate verde*): This tart green vegetable is often mistaken for a small unripe tomato when freed of its papery husk, although the two are botanically unrelated. Used as a base for many Mexican sauces and salsas. Available (preferably) fresh in the produce section or canned in the Mexican section of many supermarkets. Husk, de-stem, and wash tomatillos before use. A medium tomatillo is 1–1½ inches (2.5–3.75 cm) in diameter.

Tomato (*jitomate*): This native of Mexico and the New World is used widely in sauces and salsas; quite often roasted.

Turkey (*pavo* or *guajolote*): Popular ingredient of Yucatecan cuisine.

Vegetable pear (*chayote*): Pale green tropical squash with a sweet flavor, watery consistency, and smooth skin, resembling an Anjou pear. Its broad, flat seed is edible, but the skin of the chayote can sometimes be too tough to eat. Found in the produce section of well-stocked supermarkets. Zucchini is a passable substitute.

Zucchini squash (*calabaza*): Main ingredient of innumerable Mexican side dishes; often combined with tomato.

❧ Chiles and Mexican Cooking

The word "chile" is a mutation of "chilli," the Aztec word used to describe the New World native produce, hot peppers. Although there are probably hundreds of different types of chiles grown in Mexico, only the few described here are necessary for the purposes of this book. When a specific chile is called for in a recipe, its amount is given as a range, the lower number representing a moderate "gringo" level of piquancy and the higher number corresponding to Mexican tastes.

Remember: Always wash your hands immediately after handling chiles.

❧ Fresh Chiles/Chiles Frescos

Anaheim pepper: Also known as *chile verde* or *chile California,* this light-green mild pepper is 6–8 inches (15–20 cm) long, 1–2 inches (2.5–5 cm) in diameter, and conical at the end. It is used mostly in northern Mexico and the southwestern United States, usually roasted and peeled, then stuffed or cut into strips and used in a vegetable dish or the famous Chihuahuan dish, *chile con queso.*

Chile güero: Also known as a Hungarian wax pepper, this mild chile has a yellow or light-green skin. It is typically just a bit larger than a *chile jalapeño.*

Chile habanero: Reputed to be the hottest chile in the world, this orange, lantern-shaped chile measures a squat 2 inches (5 cm) high by 1 ½ inches (3.75 cm) in diameter. It has a unique sweet-hot flavor and is used in Mexico almost exclusively in the Yucatán peninsula. *Chile habanero* is rapidly growing in popularity in the United States via Texas.

Chile jalapeño: The best known chile in the United States, this medium- to dark-green chile measures about 2 inches (5 cm) long by 1 inch (2.5 cm) in diameter with a triangular shape. It is moderately hot and available fresh or canned (pickled *"en escabeche"*) north or south of the border. *Chile jalapeño* is also used in sauces, often as a substitute for *chile serrano.*

New Mexican green pepper: A large, mild green chile almost identical in appearance to the Anaheim pepper but reputedly superior in flavor.

Chile poblano: Probably the most popular chile in Mexico, this is the pepper used to make *chiles rellenos.* It is large and dark green, measuring 4–6 inches (10–15 cm) long and 2–3 inches (5–7.5 cm) in diameter, with a smooth skin and often irregular shape. *Chile poblano* is generally roasted and peeled and stuffed or cut into strips called *rajas*. Usually mild, it can sometimes be quite hot.

Chile serrano: Also known as *chile verde* in southern Mexico, this is the workhorse chile of Mexico and Texas. Small, slender, and green with a shiny, tough skin, it measures $1\frac{1}{2}$–2 inches (3.75–5 cm) long by $\frac{1}{4}$–$\frac{1}{2}$ inch (0.6–1.25 cm) in diameter, and ranges from hot to extremely hot. *Chile serrano* is used in sauces and salsas throughout the world of Mexican food.

∾ Dried Chiles/*Chiles Secos*

Chile ancho: The dried ripe form of the *chile poblano*, it also measures 4–6 inches (10–15 cm) long by 2–3 inches (5–7.5 cm) wide but is dark with reddish hints and a wrinkled skin. *Chile ancho* is generally toasted, soaked in water, and puréed for use in sauces.

Chile chipotle: A dried, smoked *jalapeño* that can be found canned in *adobo* (a thick, seasoned sauce) at most well-stocked supermarkets, this hot pepper imparts a smoky flavor that is utterly addictive. It measures 2–4 inches (5–10 cm) long by about 1 inch (2.5 cm) wide.

Chile de árbol: A small, bright-red chile measuring 2–3 inches (5–7.5 cm) long by about $\frac{1}{4}$ inch (0.6 cm) wide, *chile de árbol* is extremely hot and often used in table sauces. *Chile japonés,* a dried chile almost identical in appearance, is an acceptable substitute.

Chile guajillo: This maroon, smooth-skinned chile measures about 5 inches (12.5 cm) long by $1\frac{1}{2}$–2 inches (3.75–5 cm) wide. It is often combined with *chile ancho*. In Texas and northern Mexico, *chile guajillo* is sometimes called *chile cascabel,* although in most of Mexico this refers to a completely different chile. New Mexican dried red chile is an acceptable substitute.

New Mexican dried red chile: The dried ripe form of the New Mexican green chile. It is used mostly in Southwestern cuisine, but makes a passable substitute for *chile guajillo* in Mexican cooking.

Chile pasilla: Also known as *chile negro,* this slender black chile measures 6–8 inches (15–20 cm) long by 1–$1\frac{1}{2}$ inches (2.5–3.75 cm) wide, with a wrinkled skin and sweet odor. Its earthy flavor can be detected as the characteristic taste of *mole poblano,* the chocolate-chile Pueblan concoction served in many American-Mexican restaurants.

Chile piquín: A small, round, red chile known for its extreme heat level, *chile piquín* is usually ground and used as a condiment.

❧ Mexican Menus

The following suggested Mexican-style meal menus will each feed four to six people. Half of the menus feature the cuisine of a particular region of Mexico, while the others offer harmonious combinations of nonregional dishes or dishes from a number of different regions.

Make all or a portion of each meal, accompanied by the typical Mexican accouterments of salsa, warm corn or flour tortillas, lime wedges, *jalapeños en escabeche,* pickled onions, chopped fresh chile, chopped onion, chopped cilantro, and so on. If you do not have time to make all of the items of a particular menu, consider using one of these expedient but passable low-fat substitutes: canned nonfat refried beans, canned black beans, and jarred or canned salsas and pickled peppers.

❧ Regional Menus

Fiesta Guadalajara Style
Pico de Gallo a la Jalisciense/Jícama Fruit Salad
Frijoles Pintos Refritos/Refried Pinto Beans
Pozole/Hominy Soup
Aguas Frescas de Piña/Fresh Pineapple Soft Drink

Cocktails in Old Cancún
Sopa de Lima/Chicken and Lime Soup
Vuelve a la Vida/"Return to Life" Mixed Shellfish Cocktail
Salsa del Infierno/"Hot as Hell" Salsa
Cold beer or margaritas

Oaxacan Awakening
Enfrijoladas/Corn Tortillas Dipped in Bean Sauce
or *Salsa de Huevo*/Scrambled Eggs in Roasted Tomato and Chile Sauce
    with warm corn tortillas
Rajas/Strips of Roasted Green Chile and Onion
Fresh orange juice
Café de Olla/Spiced Coffee

Pochutla Pot Luck
Sopa de Nopales/Cactus Soup with Egg and Shrimp
Albóndigas Enchipotladas/Meatballs in Tomatillo-*Chipotle* Sauce
or *Enchiladas con Mole*/Chicken Enchiladas with Chile-Chocolate-Nut
    Sauce
Frijoles Negros de Olla/Pot-Boiled Black Beans

Arroz Blanco/Rice Cooked in Chicken Broth
Warm corn tortillas

Good Morning, Mérida

Arroz a la Mexicana/Mexican Rice
Huevos Motuleños/Tortillas Topped with Black Beans, Eggs, and Peas
Salsa Linda/Pretty Salsa
Cebollas a la Yucatecas/Spiced Pickled Onions
Agua de Melón/Cantaloupe Water

Comida (Lunch) a la Cuernavaca

Sopa de Habas/Fava Bean Soup
Molletes/Bean and Cheese Melts
Chayotes al Vapor/Vegetable Pear Steamed in Its Own Juices
Salsa Suave/Cool Hot Sauce

Fiesta Veracruz Style

Huachinango a la Veracruzana/Red Snapper inTomato Sauce with
    Olives and Capers
Arroz Blanco/Rice Cooked in Chicken Broth
Frijoles Pintos Refritos/Refried Pinto Beans
Warm corn tortillas

Texas Saturday Night

Baked Tortilla Chips
Salsa a la Austin
Salsa Mexicana (*Pico de Gallo*)/Classic Mexican Table Salsa
Enchiladas TexMex, Beef or Bean Burritos, or *Chipotle* Chicken Tacos
Frijoles Pintos Refritos/Refried Pinto Beans
Arroz a la Mexicana/Mexican Rice
Warm flour tortillas

Border Time

Carne Guisada/Mexican-Style Stewed Beef with warm flour tortillas or
    Fajitas/Flour Tacos Filled with Grilled Marinated Chicken or Beef
    Strips
Frijoles a la Charra/Beans with Onion, Chile, and Tomato
Calabazas Guisadas/Stewed Zucchini
Jalapeños en Escabeche/Pickled *Chiles Jalapeños* with Onion and Car-
    rots
Salsa Casera/Roasted Tomato Salsa

Supper in Puebla

Tinga de Pollo/Chipotle Chicken Stew
Arroz Blanco/Rice Cooked in Chicken Broth

Frijoles Negros de Olla/Pot-Boiled Black Beans
Agua de Jamaica/Hibiscus Soft Drink
Warm corn tortillas

Mexico City Lunch

Sopa de Pasta/Pasta in Chicken-Tomato Broth
Arroz con Plátano y Salsa/Rice with Banana
Picadillo/Mexican Minced Meat
Frijoles Pintos de Olla/Pot-Boiled Pinto Beans
Naranjada/Orange Soft Drink
Salsa Casera/Roasted Tomato Salsa
or *Salsa Mexicana* (*Pico de Gallo*)/Classic Mexican Table Salsa
Warm corn tortillas

Fiesta Chihuahua Style

Calabazas y Elotes a la Mexicana/Squash and Corn with Tomato and
  Roasted Chile
Caldillo/Brothy Beef Stew
Mixed-greens salad
Warm flour tortillas

The Streets of Zihuatanejo

Sopa de Espinacas y Coditos/Spinach and Elbow Macaroni Soup
Ensalada de Col/Mexican Cole Slaw
Enchiladas de *Camarón y Jaiba*/Shrimp and Crab Enchiladas in *Chipotle*
  Cream Sauce
Licuado de Fresa/Strawberry Fruit Shake

Acapulco Snack

Crema de Calabaza/Cream of Zucchini Soup
Ceviche/Fish in Tomato-Lime Salsa
Frijoles Negros Refritos/Refried Black Beans

The Road to Tampico

Frijoles Pintos Refritos/Refried Pinto Beans
Ostiones Guisados/Stewed Oysters
Arroz a la Mexicana/Mexican Rice
Agua de Sandía/Watermelon Water
Warm corn or flour tortillas

∾ Mealtime Menus

Breakfasts

El Número Uno

Huevos a la Mexicana/Scrambled Eggs with Onion, Chile, and Tomato
Frijoles Negros Refritos/Refried Black Beans

Salsa Verde/Tomatillo-Cilantro Green Sauce
or *Salsa Casera*/Roasted Tomato Salsa
Café con Leche/Spiced Coffee with Warmed Milk
Warm corn or flour tortillas

El Número Dos

Huevos Rancheros/Eggs on Tortillas in Tomato and Chile Sauce
Frijoles a la Charra/Beans with Onion, Chile, and Tomato
Fresh orange juice

El Número Tres

Chilaquiles Rojos/Tortilla Strips in Tomato Sauce
or *Chilaquiles Verdes con Pollo*/Tortilla Strips in Green Sauce with
     Chicken
Frijoles Negros de Olla/Pot-Boiled Black Beans
Café de Olla/Spiced Coffee

El Número Cuatro

Ensalada Tropical Especial/Tropical Fruit Salad with Yogurt and Honey
Horchata de Arroz/Rice Milk

El Número Cinco

Sopes/Corn Tortilla Pies with Salsa
Arroz a la Mexicana/Mexican Rice
Licuado de Plátano/Banana Fruit Shake

❧ Light Lunches

El Número Uno

Caldo de Pollo Especial/Deluxe Chicken Soup
Chayotes al Vapor/Vegetable Pear Steamed in Its Own Juices
Agua de Pera/Pear Water
Warm corn tortillas

El Número Dos

Arroz con Chorizo/Rice with Chile-Seasoned Meat
Quesadillas Estilo Mexico/Mexican Grilled Cheese
Salsa de Jitomate y Chile Chipotle/Tomato and Chile Chipotle Salsa

El Número Tres

Flautas
Calabazas Guisadas/Stewed Zucchini
Salsa a la Austin

El Número Cuatro

Ensalada de Chiles Rellenos/Chiles Stuffed with Tuna Salad
Sopa de Frijol Negro/Black Bean Soup

El Número Cinco

Ensalada Cesar/Caesar Salad
Caldo Tlalpeño/Chicken and Chile Chipotle Soup
Agua de Jamaica/Hibiscus Soft Drink
Crusty bread

∾ Dinners

El Número Uno

Caldo de Gato/Vegetable Soup
Mole con Pollo/Chicken in Chile-Chocolate-Nut Sauce
Cebollas Desflameadas/Mild Crisped Onions
Arroz Blanco/Rice Cooked in Chicken Broth
Agua de Melón/Cantaloupe Water
Warm corn tortillas

El Número Dos

Arroz con Pollo/Chicken with Rice
Ensalada de Ejotes/Green Bean Salad
Frijoles Negros Refritos/Refried Black Beans
Licuado de Plátano/Banana Fruit Shake
Warm flour or corn tortillas

El Número Tres

Sopa de Tortilla/Tortilla Soup
Camarones Enchipotlados/Shrimp in Chipotle Sauce
Arroz Blanco/Rice Cooked in Chicken Broth
Agua de Jamaica/Hibiscus Soft Drink

El Número Cuatro

Bud'n Azteca/Aztec Pie or Mexican Lasagna
Coliflor Poblana/Cauliflower in Spiced Tomato Sauce
Espinacas con Papas y Garbanzos/Spinach with Potatoes and Chick Peas

El Número Cinco

Enchiladas Suizas/Green Enchiladas with Cream
Arroz a la Mexicana/Mexican Rice
Papas en Salsa de Chile Pasilla/Potatoes in Chile Pasilla Sauce

Essential Cooking Equipment

In addition to the most basic kitchen equipment, such as measuring spoons, saucepans, and spatulas, only a few tools are needed to make low-fat Mexican food. The essential cooking equipment includes:

Aluminum frying pan: Great for making sauces.

Blender: Used extensively to purée, mix, and chop.

Baking dishes: A large and a medium Pyrex dish are recommended for baking enchiladas, chicken, and more.

Cast-iron frying pan: Good for toasting spices, sautéing, and cooking tortillas.

Microwave oven: Alternatives are given, but a microwave will save a lot of time, particularly when warming tortillas.

Nonstick frying pans with lids: Mandatory for any low-fat endeavor. The perfect tool for sautéing, cooking eggs, mashing refried beans, and cooking with a minimum amount of cooking oil.

Pressure cooker: Not essential, but great for making low-fat refried beans in a fraction of the time normally required.

Spice grinder or mortar and pestle: Used to grind spices.

Stock pot: Used to make beans and soups.

Strainer: Used to remove seeds and bits of vegetable skins from sauces.

Tortilla press: Necessary only if you plan to make your own tortillas. (See the chapter *"La Tortilla de Maíz*/The Corn Tortilla" for more on tortilla presses.)

Wooden bean or potato masher: Necessary for mashing refried beans, although the back of a wooden spoon can be used in a pinch. Look for one at any Mexican specialty shop.

Wooden spoons: Simply superior to metal.

Tortilla warmer: Certainly not required, since leaving tortillas in the plastic bag they were heated in or wrapping them in a dry dishtowel is sufficient for maintaining warmth and moisture, but a warmer does add to the presentation of the meal.

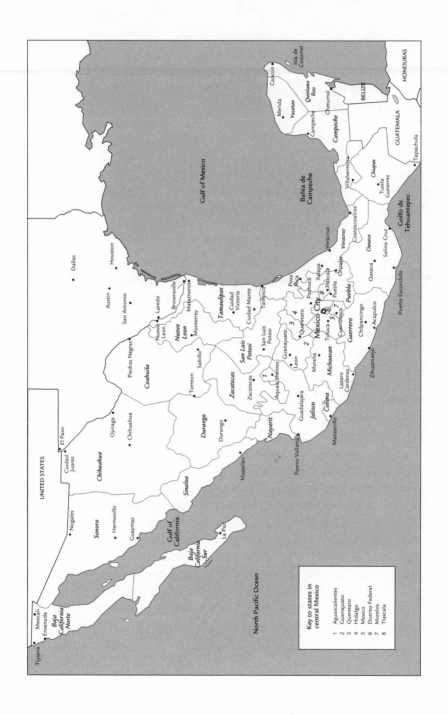

Part I

American-Mexican Cuisine

What comes to mind when you hear the words "Mexican food?" Nachos, burritos, *fajitas*, chips and salsa? It might surprise you to learn that these dishes are unknown to the majority of people living in Mexico.

American-Mexican food is based largely on the cuisine of northern Mexico, a region nearly isolated geographically from the Mexican heartland, and where far fewer people reside compared with the densely populated central and southern parts of the country. Over the years, cooks in Texas, California, New Mexico, and Arizona have used flour tortillas, beef, Jack cheese, Anaheim peppers, pinto beans, and other ingredients prevalent in Mexico's northern states to create their own distinctive versions of "Mexican" food. At the same time, southwestern United States' incarnations of such national Mexican standards as tamales, tacos, and enchiladas have evolved, often reflecting northern Mexican nuances.

The result of this culinary migration is a style of food that is Mexican in concept but very much American in practice. From grilled *flautas* to frozen margaritas, this north-of-the-border fare has become a bona fide part of our country's cuisine. And as the American-Mexican food explosion continues, new Southwestern, Californian, and TexMex regional ingredients, climates, and cooks promise to further redefine the United States' Mexican cuisine.

Chapter 2

Gringo Grub: America's Mexican Food

From California burritos to Texas enchiladas, many standard American-Mexican dishes have achieved a prominence equal to that of hamburgers, hot dogs, and pizza in the United States. And despite regional styles and specialties, a number of dishes have emerged to form what might be called the core of American-Mexican cuisine. Chips and salsa, *fajitas, quesadillas, nachos, chiles rellenos*—these are just some of the staples of Mexican food as it is known in the United States.

Unfortunately, as the Center for Science in the Public Interest confirmed in 1994, a typical plate of the Mexican food served in the United States isn't any healthier than a cheeseburger or chili dog. From oil-soaked *tostadas* to greasy taco salads, American-Mexican restaurants offer little for the fat-conscious diner. Fortunately, it is possible to create light but tasty Mexican food at home.

In the following pages you will find low-fat renditions of a number of classic American-Mexican dishes. The recipes are practical and straightforward, including light versions of *nachos*, burritos, enchiladas, tacos, *fajitas, chile rellenos*, and *flautas*. In addition, at the end of each recipe in this chapter, you will also find references to related low-fat traditional Mexican dishes found in this book. Thus, you can learn how to prepare your favorite American-Mexican items at a fraction of the fat they normally contain, and also, you can begin to explore Mexico's food through familiar flavors and ingredients.

❧ Salsa a la Austin

Yield: About 2 cups (500 ml)

One of the pleasures of dining in Austin, Texas, whether at a café or TexMex restaurant, is knowing that an endless supply of chips and a salsa like this one will be on your table before you sit down.

Ingredients

1 can stewed tomatoes, 14.5 oz (406 g)
½ clove garlic, minced
¼ cup (60 ml) finely chopped white onion
1–2 *chiles serranos* or *jalapeños*, finely chopped
¼ teaspoon salt, or to taste
½ teaspoon fresh lime juice
Pinch of ground cumin
Freshly ground black pepper (optional)
⅓ cup (80 ml) chopped cilantro, loosely packed

Preparation

Put the tomatoes, garlic, onion, chiles, and salt in a blender and pulse-blend to mix only. Do not purée as the salsa should have a thick, textured consistency. Pour the salsa into a nonmetallic bowl. Add the lime juice, cumin, and black pepper, and mix well. Stir in cilantro and chill in the refrigerator for 10 minutes to season. Serve.

Variations

There are many variations of this salsa, as it lends itself to experimentation. You may omit the lime, cumin, and/or cilantro, or add more of each plus diced steamed carrots, bell pepper, scallion greens, and so on.

❧ Tips

You can store this salsa in the refrigerator in a covered glass jar for up to two weeks.

❧ South of the Border

The traditional Mexican counterpart to this tomato-based salsa is *Salsa Casera* (page 73).

Nutrition Information
Serving: ½ cup (125 ml)
Amounts per Serving

Calories: 66
Calories from fat: 4.9%
Total fat: 0.4 g
Saturated fat: 0 g

Cholesterol: 0 mg
Carbohydrates: 15.6 g
Protein: 3.1 g
Sodium: 442 mg

～ Raw Tomatillo Salsa

Yield: 2 cups (500 ml)

This attractive salsa is good with burritos, enchiladas, eggs, and tacos of any sort. Of course, it's a wonderful dip for baked tortilla chips as well.

Ingredients

1–3 large *chiles jalapeños*, finely chopped
$\frac{1}{4}$ teaspoon salt, or to taste
Pinch of sugar
$\frac{1}{4}$ cup (60 ml) cold water
8 medium tomatillos, about $\frac{3}{4}$ pound (300 g), with the husks and
   stems removed
2 tablespoons chopped avocado

Preparation

Put chiles, salt, sugar, and water in a blender and blend until smooth. Quarter tomatillos; add them to the blender and blend coarsely, leaving some texture in the sauce. Add the avocado and purée. Chill in the refrigerator for 10 minutes. Serve.

Variations

If you're just nuts about cilantro, add 2 tablespoons chopped cilantro to the blender with the chiles, salt, and water.

～ Tips

This salsa is best eaten freshly made.

～ South of the Border

One of the most common salsas in Mexico is the tomatillo sauce, *Salsa Verde* (page 71).

Nutrition Information
Serving: ½ cup (60 ml)
Amounts per Serving

Calories: 47	Cholesterol: 0 mg
Calories from fat: 25.3%	Carbohydrates: 7.7 g
Total fat: 1.4 g	Protein: 1.4 g
Saturated fat: 0.2 g	Sodium: 137 mg

❧ Baked Tortilla Chips

Yield: 20–25 chips

Virtually all of the fat and calories of a normal serving of chips and salsa come from the frying process. Not only does baking your own chips convert this American-Mexican favorite into a low-fat snack, it's also a great way to use up stale tortillas.

Ingredients
6 white corn tortillas, 5 inches (12.5 cm) in diameter
Salt

Preparation
Preheat oven to 325°F (160°C). Pass each tortilla through running water, shake off excess water, and sprinkle each side liberally with salt. Stack the salted tortillas and cut them into quarters. Separate the quarters, lay them flat on an ungreased cookie sheet, and bake for 20–25 minutes until crisp. Serve, or store in a zipper-lock plastic bag.

❧ Tips
To feed a crowd, double the recipe and heat chips on two cookie sheets.

❧ South of the Border
Tortillas and salsa are combined in a whole new way in *Chilaquiles Rojos* (pages 196–197).

Nutrition Information
Serving: About 12 chips
Amounts per Serving

Calories: 166
Calories from fat: 9.8%
Total fat: 1.9 g
Saturated fat: 0.2 g

Cholesterol: 0 mg
Carbohydrates: 35 g
Protein: 4.3 g
Sodium: 653 mg

∾ Black Bean Dip

Yield: About 2 cups (500 ml)

This creamy nonfat dip is a nice change of pace when you're just not in a salsa mood. Or serve it along with a hot sauce or two for the consummate American-Mexican appetizer.

Ingredients

1 ½ cups (375 ml) *Frijoles Negros de Olla* (page 132) or 1 can black beans, 15 oz (420 g), drained
¼ cup (60 ml) canned nacho *jalapeño* slices, finely chopped
1 tablespoon minced bell pepper
1 teaspoon minced onion
1 ½ teaspoons cider vinegar
1 teaspoon chile powder
¼ teaspoon ground cumin
¼ teaspoon garlic powder
¼ teaspoon salt, or to taste

Preparation

Put all ingredients in a blender and purée. Pour the contents of the blender into a glass jar, cover, and chill in the refrigerator for 30 minutes. Serve with baked tortilla chips.

∾ Tips

Add more or less vinegar to adjust the tartness of the dip.

∾ South of the Border

If you enjoy the incomparable flavor of puréed black beans, check out *Enfrijoladas* (pages 194–195), *Sopa de Frijol Negro* (page 173), and *Chiles Rellenos de Arroz Integral* (pages 110–111).

Nutrition Information
Serving: ¼ cup (60 ml) with 10 baked tortilla chips
Amounts per Serving

Calories: 184
Calories from fat: 7%
Total fat: 1.4 g
Saturated fat: 0.1 g

Cholesterol: 0 mg
Carbohydrates: 36.3 g
Protein: 6.8 g
Sodium: 329 mg

❧ American-Mexican *Quesadillas*

Yield: 5 servings as a snack

These Mexican grilled cheese sandwiches make a delicious snack or appetizer.

Ingredients

2 cups (500 ml) finely chopped button mushrooms
2 tablespoons chopped scallion greens
Salt, to taste
2 cups (500 ml) shredded reduced-fat mozzarella cheese
10 light flour tortillas
1 cup (250 ml) of your favorite salsa
1 sprig fresh cilantro as a garnish

Preparation

Coat a nonstick frying pan with cooking spray and heat over medium heat. Add mushrooms and scallion greens and cook for 2 minutes. Remove from heat and allow to cool for 10 minutes. Transfer to a bowl, add salt and cheese, and mix well.

Lay 5 flour tortillas on the counter. Spread a handful—about ½ cup (60 ml)—of the mushroom mixture on each. Top each cheese-covered tortilla with one of the 5 remaining tortillas. Spray a large nonstick frying pan well with cooking spray and heat over medium heat. Lay one *quesadilla* on the pan, cover, and cook for 2–2½ minutes until the facedown side is speckled brown. Press the *quesadilla* with a spatula, flip, and cook for 1½ minutes, covered, until the other side is similarly speckled.

Repeat this cooking process for remaining *quesadillas*. Keep cooked *quesadillas* stacked, wrapped in a dry dishtowel, until they all are cooked. Using a pizza cutter or sharp knife, cut each into four wedges. Garnish with a sprig of fresh cilantro and serve, accompanied by salsa.

Variations

There is no end to possible *quesadilla* fillings: shredded chicken, chile, crab meat, *rajas*, tomatoes, and so on.

❧ Tips

To make *quesadillas* faster, cook several simultaneously in two or three pans.

❧ South of the Border

Mexican *quesadillas*—Quesadillas *Estilo Mexico* (pages 183–184)—are made with corn tortillas.

Nutrition Information
Serving: 1 quesadilla
Amounts per Serving

Calories: 244

Cholesterol: 24 mg

Calories from fat: 20.8%

Carbohydrates: 33.5 g

Total fat: 6.1 g

Protein: 19 g

Saturated fat: 3.2 g

Sodium: 882 mg

∾ Migas
Scrambled Eggs with Tomatoes, Chiles, and Tortilla Chips

Yield: 4 servings

Literally "scraps," *Migas* is one of the most popular breakfasts in Texas, and one that usually wins visitors over after just one bite. Serve accompanied by light flour tortillas and plenty of salsa.

Ingredients

2 medium eggs
1½ cups (375 ml) egg substitute
2 teaspoons corn oil
½ large white onion, chopped
1–3 *chiles serranos*, finely chopped
1 large tomato, seeded and chopped
15 baked tortilla chips, commercial or homemade
¼ cup (60 ml) shredded reduced-fat cheddar cheese

Preparation

Mix the eggs and egg substitute in a bowl and set aside. Heat the corn oil in a large nonstick frying pan or a sauté pan over medium heat. Add the onion and chile and sauté until the onion is soft but not brown, about 3 minutes. Add the tomato and heat 1 minute, stirring frequently.

Increase the heat to medium-high and add the egg mixture to the pan. Cook for 4–5 minutes, stirring occasionally, until the eggs begin to set. Add chips and mix well. Cook for 3 minutes, stirring frequently. Sprinkle the cheese over eggs and tortillas, cover, and heat for 1 minute. Remove the pan from the heat and leave undisturbed for 2–3 minutes. Serve.

Variations

Since *Migas* is a throw-together dish, there are no limits to the ingredients you can add to the sauté: mushrooms, spinach, bell peppers, artichoke hearts, black olives, and so on.

∾ South of the Border

For more Mexican egg dishes, see the chapter *"Desayunos*/Breakfasts."

Nutrition Information
Amounts per Serving

Calories: 170   Cholesterol: 112 mg
Calories from fat: 33.7%   Carbohydrates: 18.6 g
Total fat: 6.5 g   Protein: 10.0 g
Saturated fat: 1.8 g   Sodium: 234 mg

⁓ Nachos

Yield: 4–6 servings as an appetizer

Normally, a helping of these all-American munchies glistens with grease, but a serving of this slimmed-down version contains about the same amount of fat as a cup of yogurt.

Ingredients

1½ cups (375 ml) *Frijoles Refritos* (pages 134–135) or 1 can nonfat refried beans, 15 oz (420 g)

3 tablespoons water

12 white corn tortillas, 5 inches (12.5 cm) in diameter

¾ cup (185 ml) grated reduced-fat mozzarella cheese

½ cup (125 ml) grated reduced-fat cheddar cheese

1 jar nacho *jalapeño* slices, 12 oz (336 g), drained

2 cups (500 ml) *Salsa Mexicana* (page 70) as a garnish (optional)

Preparation

Put the beans in a bowl, thin with 3 tablespoons of water, and set aside. Preheat oven to 325°F (160°C). Pass each tortilla through running water and shake off the excess water. Stack the wet tortillas and cut into halves or quarters. Separate the quarters and arrange them on two cookie sheets sprayed lightly with nonfat cooking spray, overlapping pieces as little as possible.

Bake the tortillas for 15–20 minutes until just crisp. Remove the chips from the oven, combine on one cookie sheet, and cover completely with beans. Sprinkle with mozzarella, then cheddar cheese. Top with *jalapeño* slices to taste. Bake for 10 minutes. Remove and serve on a large plate or platter, accompanied by *Salsa Mexicana*.

Nutrition Information
Amounts per Serving

Calories: 238	Cholesterol: 2 mg
Calories from fat: 18.8%	Carbohydrates: 36.2 g
Total fat: 5.1 g	Protein: 13.9 g
Saturated fat: 2.3 g	Sodium: 1,020 mg

❧ Tacos

Tacos are the ultimate finger food. Made with corn or flour tortillas as the "bread," these Mexican sandwiches are renowned on both sides of the border as informal, inexpensive fare. Making a taco is simple: Place a few tablespoons of meat, beans, vegetables, or other filling on a warm tortilla; fold the tortilla and cover the filling with salsa, lime, shredded lettuce or cabbage, cheese, and so on. The result is an instant hand-to-mouth meal that becomes a hearty feast when served with rice and/or beans.

The following recipes are a few distinctive American-Mexican creations, but remember that just about anything can be used as a filling for tacos. Vegetarians in particular should keep this in mind, as most of the side dishes in the chapter *"Platos al Lado/Side Dishes"* make wonderful taco dinners when served with tortillas, rice, and beans.

❧ Black Bean Tacos

Yield: 4 servings

Ingredients
3 cups (750 ml) *Frijoles de Ollas Negros* (page 132) or 2 cans black
    beans, 15 oz (420 g) each, with broth
8 light flour tortillas
½ cup (125 ml) shredded reduced-fat cheddar cheese
1 ½ cups (375 ml) *Salsa Mexicana* (page 70)
1 ½ cups (375 ml) *Salsa del Infierno* (page 80)
Chopped fresh cilantro as a garnish
Salsa del Infierno (page 80) as a garnish

Preparation
Make tacos two at a time. Heat the beans in a saucepan over medium heat until the broth is thick, then remove it from the heat. Heat two tortillas in a hot nonstick frying pan over medium-high heat for 20 seconds per side or in the microwave for 35 seconds.

Place the tortillas on a plate. Put a couple of spoonfuls of beans and 2 tablespoons of cheese on the center of each. Top with *Salsa Mexicana, Salsa del Infierno*, or bottled *habanero* hot sauce and plenty of fresh cilantro. Fold and serve.

Variations
Add baked chicken bites (as for Chicken Burritos, page 57) for an extra-special filling.

Calories: 352

Calories from fat: 12.0%

Total fat: 5.0 g

Saturated fat: 2.5 g

Cholesterol: 12 mg

Carbohydrates: 62.8 g

Protein: 19.5 g

Sodium: 657 mg

✐ Potato and Egg Breakfast Tacos

Yield: 6 servings

Ingredients

1½ pounds (¾ kg) new potatoes, peeled
Salt, to taste
4 eggs
1 cup (250 ml) egg substitute
1 medium tomato, seeded and chopped (optional)
12 light flour tortillas
½ cup (125 ml) shredded reduced-fat cheddar or Monterey Jack
   cheese
Salsa as a garnish
Nacho *jalapeño* slices as a garnish

Preparation

Boil potatoes for 25–30 minutes in plenty of water until soft throughout. Drain, rinse well with cold water, let cool, and dice. Heat oil in a large nonstick frying pan over medium heat. Add potatoes and cook for 5–10 minutes, stirring occasionally, until lightly browned. Season with salt.

Meanwhile, beat eggs and mix well with the egg substitute. Remove the lid from the frying pan, add the tomato, and heat for 1 minute. Add the eggs, stir, and heat about 5 minutes until the eggs are cooked.

Warm the flour tortillas as described on page 20. Set the egg-potato mixture, cheese, salsa, and *jalapeños* on the table in separate bowls and allow individuals to create their own tacos.

Variations

There are many other breakfast taco ingredients in addition to the popular filling of potato and egg. Refried beans, any kind of rice, and *chorizo* (pages 139–140) all work well.

Nutrition Information
Amounts per Serving

Calories: 344	Cholesterol: 150 mg
Calories from fat: 21%	Carbohydrates: 54.4 g
Total fat: 8.5 g	Protein: 17.4 g
Saturated fat: 3.1 g	Sodium: 829 mg

∾ *Chipotle* Chicken Tacos

Yield: 4–6 servings

Ingredients

3 split chicken breasts
2 teaspoons corn oil
½ medium white onion, chopped
1 large ripe tomato, chopped, or 1 can whole tomatoes, 14 oz (392 g),
    drained and chopped
2–4 canned *chiles chipotles* in *adobo*, finely chopped
¼ teaspoon ground cumin
Salt, to taste
12 light flour or corn tortillas
Chopped green leaf lettuce as a garnish

Preparation

Poach and shred the chicken as described on page 19. Heat the oil in a
nonstick frying pan over medium heat. Add the chopped onion and sauté
3–5 minutes until soft but not brown. Add the tomato and heat for 1–2
minutes. Add chiles, plus some *adobo* if a spicy sauce is desired, and simmer for 1 minute.

Add the chicken, stir, season with cumin and salt, and heat through.
Warm the tortillas as described on page 20. Fill each tortilla with ¼ cup
(60 ml) of the chicken and top with lettuce. Serve with *Frijoles Refritos*
(pages 134–135), *Frijoles Negros de Olla* (pages 132–133), or *Frijoles a la
Charra* (page 136).

Nutrition Information
Amounts per Serving

Calories: 302
Calories from fat: 14.9%
Total fat: 5.4 g
Saturated fat: 1.5 g

Cholesterol: 49 mg
Carbohydrates: 43.9 g
Protein: 25.5 g
Sodium: 949 mg

❧ Enchiladas

Stuffed corn tortillas that are literally "chile-ed," or seasoned in chile sauce, enchiladas are the quintessential Mexican creation. Not only do they contain two of the Big Three ingredients of Mexican food—corn and chile—but having evolved as a use for stale tortillas, they also epitomize the creative economy of the Mexican kitchen. Fittingly, enchiladas may be the most popular Mexican dish in the world.

Although styles vary, preparing enchiladas commonly consists of softening corn tortillas, then filling, rolling, and baking them. Finally, they are dressed with a savory sauce and fresh toppings. Ordinarily, the first of these steps involves passing each tortilla through hot oil—and straight to Fat City. Fortunately, this grease treatment can be avoided by using water instead of oil to process the tortillas.

Rolling Enchiladas the Low-Fat Way

Only a few items are necessary to roll enchiladas: a large baking dish (or two small ones), a nonstick frying pan or a microwave oven and a zipper-lock plastic bag, corn tortillas, and an enchilada filling (recipes follow).

Softening the Tortilla

To soften tortillas in a nonstick pan, heat the pan over medium-high heat. Pass a corn tortilla under running water; shake off any excess water. Lay the tortilla in the pan and heat for 20–30 seconds without disturbing until steam begins to escape from underneath the tortilla. Flip the tortilla over and heat 10–20 seconds until steam escapes and the tortilla is warm and soft. Remove the tortilla, let it cool until it can be handled, and then roll it immediately.

To soften tortillas in a microwave, put 5–10 corn tortillas in a plastic zipper-lock bag, sprinkle with $\frac{1}{4}$ teaspoon water, seal, and heat for 60 seconds until the tortillas are soft and moist. Remove and roll tortillas one at a time, sealing the bag each time one is removed.

Rolling the Tortilla

Lay the softened tortilla on a plate. Place about $\frac{1}{4}$ cup (60 ml) of the enchilada filling on it, towards one end. Roll the tortilla up tightly, starting at the end with the filling. Lay the rolled tortilla in the baking dish "seam" down, snug against its neighbor or the wall of the dish. Repeating the softening and rolling procedures, fill the dish to capacity. The enchiladas are now ready for baking.

❧ TexMex Enchiladas

Yield: 4 servings

Ingredients

Salsa Verde Cocida or *Salsa Ranchera* (recipes follow)
3 large split chicken breasts
14 white corn tortillas, 5 inches (12.5 cm) in diameter
1 ½ cups or 6 oz (375 ml or 170 g) shredded reduced-fat mozzarella
  cheese

Preparation

Prepare *Salsa Verde Cocida* or *Salsa Ranchera*. Poach and shred the chicken breast as described on page 19. Preheat oven to 375°F (190°C). Roll the tortillas into enchiladas (page 49), filling each with ¼ cup (60 ml) of shredded chicken. Bake for 10 minutes.

Warm *Salsa Verde Cocida* or *Salsa Ranchera* in a medium saucepan. Remove the enchiladas from the oven, cover completely with salsa, then cheese. Place under the broiler for 1–2 minutes until the cheese is completely melted. Remove, allow enchiladas to cool for 5–10 minutes, and serve.

Nutrition Information
Amounts per Serving with *Salsa Verde*

Calories: 511
Calories from fat: 19.6%
Total fat: 11.2 g
Saturated fat: 3.3 g

Cholesterol: 84 mg
Carbohydrates: 57.8 g
Protein: 45.9 g
Sodium: 1,070 mg

~ Salsa Verde Cocida

Ingredients

15–18 tomatillos, 1½ pounds (¾ kg)
2–4 *chiles jalapeños*
2 cups (500 ml) water
2 teaspoons olive oil
2 thick slices white onion
3 cloves garlic
½ teaspoon salt

Preparation

Remove the husks and stems from the tomatillos. Remove the stems from the *chiles jalapeños*. Put tomatillos, chiles, and 2 cups (500 ml) water in a large saucepan and simmer for 5–8 minutes until tomatillos are soft, then mash them in the cooking water and simmer for 2–3 minutes longer. Remove from the heat and allow them to cool for 5–10 minutes.

Heat the oil in a large frying pan over medium heat. Add one onion slice and blacken. Meanwhile, put the remaining onion slice, garlic, and salt in a blender. Add enough tomatillo mixture to fill the blender and blend until smooth. Pour into a large bowl. Add the remainder of the tomatillo mixture to the blender, blend until smooth, and add to the bowl. Mix the two batches together well.

Remove the blackened onion from the frying pan and discard. Add the contents of blender to the pan, stir, and simmer about 10 minutes, stirring occasionally, until the sauce thickens. Let the sauce cool at least 5 minutes before use. This sauce will keep for up to a week stored in the refrigerator in a covered glass jar.

∾ Salsa Ranchera

Ingredients

6 medium ripe tomatoes (2 pounds or 1 kg) or 1 can each whole
   tomatoes, 28 oz (784 g) and 14.5 oz (406 g)
2–8 *chile serranos*, stems removed
2 slices white onion, ⅛-inch (½-cm) thick each
3 cloves garlic, chopped
½ teaspoon salt
2 teaspoons corn oil

Preparation

Broil and peel the fresh tomatoes and chiles as described on pages 18–19,
and allow to cool. Put one onion slice, the garlic, chiles, and salt in a blender.
Add broiled tomatoes or one canned tomatoes plus their juice and blend
until smooth.

Heat the oil in an aluminum or nonstick frying pan over medium heat.
Add the remaining onion slice and blacken. Remove and discard the onion, and lower the heat to medium-low.

Add the contents of the blender to the pan and simmer for 5–10 minutes, stirring occasionally, until the sauce has thickened. Allow the sauce
to cool at least 5 minutes before use. This sauce will keep for up to ten days
stored in the refrigerator in a covered glass jar.

∾ South of the Border

In addition to these American-Mexican recipes, you will find traditional
Mexican enchilada dishes in the chapter *"Platos Fuertes*/Main Dishes."

∾ Ricotta Cheese and *Chile Poblano* Enchiladas

Yield: 6 servings

Ingredients

2 large *chiles poblanos*
5 large ripe tomatoes
2–5 *chiles serranos*
3 cloves garlic
1 tablespoon corn oil
½ teaspoon salt
20 white corn tortillas, 5 inches (12.5 cm) in diameter
2 containers nonfat ricotta cheese, 14 oz (392 g) each
Cebollas Desflameadas/Mild Crisped Onions (page 84)

Preparation

Roast and peel *chiles poblanos* as described on page 19. Slit each roasted chile down one side and remove the stem, veins, and seeds. Cut the flesh into thin strips and set aside. Put tomatoes and *chiles serranos* in a large saucepan and cover with water. Bring to a boil, lower the heat, and simmer for 4–6 minutes until soft. Strain; reserve cooking water.

Put garlic, boiled *chiles serranos*, and ¾ cups (185 ml) chile cooking water in a blender and blend 5 seconds. Peel the tomatoes, add to the blender, and blend coarsely for about 20 seconds. Heat the oil in an aluminum frying pan over medium heat. Add the contents of blender and simmer for 15 minutes; season with salt. Preheat oven to 375°F (190°C). Roll tortillas into enchiladas (page 49), filling each with ¼ cup (60 ml) ricotta cheese and 3 strips of *chile poblano*.

Bake enchiladas for 8 minutes. Remove, cover completely with two-thirds of the tomato sauce, top with two-thirds of the onions, and bake 5 minutes longer. Remove and serve, topping each serving with a few tablespoons of the remaining tomato sauce and onion.

Nutrition Information
Amounts per Serving

Calories: 580	Cholesterol: 7 mg
Calories from fat: 14.5%	Carbohydrates: 52.5 g
Total fat: 4.4 g	Protein: 6.4 g
Saturated fat: 0.6 g	Sodium: 414 mg

∾ Mushroom Enchiladas

Yield: 4–6 servings

Ingredients

1 teaspoon corn oil
1 tablespoon butter
½ cup (125 ml) minced white onion
2 cloves garlic, minced
1–2 *chiles serranos*, finely chopped
2 pounds (1 kg) mushrooms, quartered
2 tablespoons chopped cilantro
Pinch of salt
18 white corn tortillas, 5 inches (12.5 cm) in diameter
Salsa Verde Cocida (page 51)
¾ cup (185 ml) shredded reduced-fat Monterey Jack or cheddar
   cheese

Preparation

Heat the oil and butter in a frying pan over medium heat. Add the onion, garlic, and chiles and sauté for 3–5 minutes until the onion is soft but not brown. Add mushrooms, cover, and cook for 8–10 minutes over low heat until tender, stirring occasionally. Remove the lid, increase the heat to medium, and cook uncovered about 20 minutes until most of the moisture in the pan has evaporated. Add the cilantro, mix well, and heat for 1 minute. Season with salt and remove from heat.

Preheat oven to 375°F (190°C). One by one, roll tortillas into enchiladas (page 49), filling each with ¼ cup (60 ml) of cooled mushroom mixture. Bake enchiladas for 10 minutes. Meanwhile, warm *Salsa Verde Cocida* in a medium saucepan. Remove the enchiladas from the oven, cover completely with sauce, sprinkle with cheese, and place under the broiler for 1–2 minutes. Serve.

∾ Tips

Serve with a garnish of nonfat or light sour cream and chopped tomato.

Nutrition Information
Amounts per Serving

Calories: 422	Cholesterol: 15 mg
Calories from fat: 22.0%	Carbohydrates: 69.7 g
Total fat: 11.0 g	Protein: 18.1 g
Saturated fat: 3.1 g	Sodium: 646 mg

❧ Burritos

Prevalent in the United States but unknown in most of Mexico, burritos may be the original take-out victuals. Legend has it that workers in northern Mexico carried packets of simple soul food wrapped in large flour tortillas to eat during lengthy commutes aboard small donkeys, or burros. Over time, convenience and simple preparation helped the burrito, or "little burro," become a definitive dish of American-Mexican cuisine. Not only are burritos an increasingly popular order at drive-through windows across the United States, but they also make for a quick, economical meal at home.

Creating a healthy burrito is largely prep work. Prepare and set aside all the desired toppings. Set aside as many extra-large (9- to 10-inch or 22.5- to 25-cm) flour tortillas as the number of burritos you plan to make. Cook the desired fillings and immediately begin to fill and roll the tortillas one by one. Once rolled, the burritos may be eaten using a knife and fork or simply by hand.

Rolling a Burrito

Rolling a burrito is not difficult, but like many things, it takes one or two attempts to get the hang of it.

Heat an extra-large (preferably low-fat) flour tortilla in a hot nonstick or cast-iron frying pan for about 20 seconds per side or in the microwave for 45 seconds. Lay the warm tortilla on a large plate. Spoon about $\frac{1}{2}$ cup (125 ml) of the desired filling (recipes follow) onto the side closer to you and spread it over roughly half of the tortilla, leaving some space near the edges of the tortilla to fold the ends in. Add the desired toppings.

Fold the tortilla's left and right ends in towards the center; then roll it up, beginning at the side with the filling and toppings. As you roll, the left- and right-end flaps should remain tucked in and straight. Place the burrito seam down on the plate. Heat for 5–10 minutes in a 325°F (160°C) oven or for 20 seconds in the microwave, and serve. If you're preparing several burritos, heat them all at once immediately before serving.

Toppings

The key to making a burrito to order is having an assortment of tasty toppings ready to add to the basic filling immediately before rolling. Although there is no limit to possible accouterments, some common healthy goodies to have on hand include:

Shredded lettuce
Seeded and chopped tomato
Finely chopped onion or scallion

Chopped fresh cilantro
Reduced-fat cheddar or Monterey Jack cheese
Light or nonfat sour cream thinned with skim milk
Salsa or salsas
Nacho *jalapeño* slices
Boiled white or brown rice

~ Bean Burritos

Yield: 3–4 burritos

This and the following other fillings will make substantial burritos and should be used immediately after their preparation. Feel free to modify the recipes or experiment with other low-fat fillings that might taste good nestled in a flour tortilla blanket.

Ingredients

1 ½ cups (375 ml) *Frijoles Refritos* (pages 134–135) or 1 can nonfat
   refried beans, 15 oz (420 g)
2 tablespoons water

Preparation

Put the beans in the saucepan, thin with water, and warm over medium-low heat.

Variations

Bean and Sausage Burrito: Sauté a cup or two of *chorizo* (pages 139–140) and stir it in with the refried beans.

Nutrition Information
Amounts per Serving (not including toppings)

Calories: 367	Cholesterol: 12 mg
Calories from fat: 16.8%	Carbohydrates: 57.4 g
Total fat: 6.8 g	Protein: 17.6 g
Saturated fat: 1.6 g	Sodium: 581 mg

∾ Chicken Burritos

Yield: 4 burritos

Ingredients
4 skinless, boneless chicken breasts
2 cloves garlic, crushed
1 lime, quartered

Preparation
Preheat oven to 400°F (205°C). Rinse the chicken with water and pat dry. Rub with garlic, then lime. Put the chicken in a baking dish sprayed lightly with cooking spray. Bake for 10 minutes, turn the breasts over, and continue to bake about 10 minutes until the meat is cooked but still moist. Remove the chicken. When cool enough to handle, cut it into bite-size chunks or strips.

Nutrition Information
Amounts per Serving (not including toppings)

Calories: 279
Calories from fat: 18.3%
Total fat: 5.5 g
Saturated fat: 0.4 g

Cholesterol: 51 mg
Carbohydrates: 30.6 g
Protein: 24.7 g
Sodium: 60 mg

ꝏ Beef Burritos

Yield: 6 burritos

Ingredients

2 teaspoons olive oil
1 medium white onion, finely chopped
2 large cloves garlic, finely chopped
1 pound (½ kg) extra-lean ground beef
1 ½ teaspoons chili powder
½ teaspoon ground cumin
1 cup (250 ml) or 4 oz (100 g) tomato sauce
Salt, to taste

Preparation

Heat the oil in a nonstick frying pan over medium heat. Add the onion and garlic, and sauté for 3–5 minutes until the onion is soft but not brown. Add the meat and brown for 2–4 minutes. Add the spices, cook for 2 minutes, and stir in tomato sauce. Reduce the heat to medium and heat for 5 minutes until the sauce has the consistency of gravy. Season with salt and allow to cool for 2–3 minutes.

Nutrition Information
Amounts per Serving (not including toppings)

Calories: 291
Calories from fat: 30.8%
Total fat: 9.0 g
Saturated fat: 1.5 g

Cholesterol: 37 mg
Carbohydrates: 33.1 g
Protein: 12.6 g
Sodium: 433 mg

∿ Veggie Burritos

Yield: 6 burritos

Ingredients

1 tablespoon olive oil
1 medium white onion
3 cloves garlic, finely chopped
½ large bell pepper, chopped
2 carrots, finely chopped
5 large button mushrooms, chopped
1 medium ripe tomato, seeded and chopped
1 cup (250 ml) chopped zucchini squash
1 cup (250 ml) chopped yellow squash
¼ teaspoon ground cumin
Salt, to taste
1 can red kidney beans, 15 oz (420 g), drained
½ cup (125 ml) shredded reduced-fat mozzarella cheese

Preparation

Heat the oil in large nonstick frying pan or sauté pan over medium-high heat. Add the onion, garlic, and bell pepper, and sauté for 5 minutes until the onion is soft. Add carrots, mushrooms, and tomato, and mix. Cover the pan, lower the heat to medium, and cook for 5 minutes.

Remove the lid, add zucchini and yellow squash, and mix. Cover the pan and continue to cook for 7 minutes until carrots are tender. Remove the lid, stir in cumin, and season with salt. Add beans and mix well. Increase the heat to medium-high and cook uncovered for 2–3 minutes until most of moisture in the pan is gone.

Sprinkle cheese over the vegetables, cover the pan, and remove from the heat. Leave undisturbed for 3 minutes; then remove the lid, mix the cheese and vegetables together, and allow to set about 5 minutes.

Nutrition Information
Amounts per Serving (not including toppings)

Calories: 247	Cholesterol: 5 mg
Calories from fat: 27.0%	Carbohydrates: 36.1 g
Total fat: 7.4 g	Protein: 8.7 g
Saturated fat: 0.8 g	Sodium: 172 mg

✎ Fajitas/Flour Tacos Filled with Grilled, Marinated Chicken or Beef Strips

Yield: 4–6 servings

Fajitas were invented in northern Mexico but perfected in Texas, where there are as many variations as there are barbecue pits. This recipe was given to me by Laredo native Ubaldo Granados.

Ingredients

1 teaspoon (if using beef) or ½ teaspoon (if using chicken) meat tenderizer
2 teaspoons lemon pepper
Juice of two limes
1 bottle lager beer, 12 oz (336 g)
1½ pound (¾ kg) skirt, or flank, steak or boneless, skinless chicken breast
1 teaspoon olive oil
½ medium white onion, cut into thin strips
1 bell pepper, seeded and cut into thin strips
8–12 nonfat (if using beef) or low-fat (if using chicken) flour tortillas
½ cup nonfat sour cream thinned with 2 tablespoons skim milk
Shredded reduced-fat cheddar cheese as a garnish
Shredded green leaf lettuce as a garnish
Salsa Mexicana (page 70) as a garnish

Preparation

Put the tenderizer, lemon pepper, lime juice, and beer in a gallon-size (3.75-liter) zipper-lock bag and mix. Put the beef or chicken between two pieces of wax paper or plastic wrap and pound the meat lightly with the bottom of a thick glass (or roll it using a rolling pin) to a thickness of ½–1 inch (1.25–2.5 cm). Remove the wax paper and put the beef or chicken in the bag with the marinade and seal. Marinate in the refrigerator for 12–24 hours.

Heat the oil in a large nonstick frying pan over medium-high heat. Add the onion and bell pepper, cover, and cook about 5 minutes until the onion is soft and the pepper begins to blacken. Transfer the vegetables to a bowl, cover, and set aside.

Drain the meat and broil or grill. To broil, put the chicken or beef on a broiler pan and broil 2–3 inches (5–7.5 cm) from the flame for 4–6 minutes or until the meat is cooked through. To grill, barbecue the meat for 4–6 minutes per side or until done. Slice the chicken or beef across the grain into ½-inch-thick (1.25-cm) strips.

Warm the tortillas as described on page 20. Arrange the meat on a large platter and serve, accompanied by sour cream, cheese, lettuce, and salsa, and allow individuals to create their own *fajita* tacos.

Nutrition Information: Chicken *Fajitas*
Amounts per Serving

Calories: 365
Calories from fat: 13.2%
Total fat: 5.2 g
Saturated fat: 1.5 g

Cholesterol: 82 mg
Carbohydrates: 40.7 g
Protein: 37.0 g
Sodium: 879 mg

Nutrition Information: Beef *Fajitas*
Amounts per Serving

Calories: 455
Calories from fat: 35.0%
Total fat: 15.5 g
Saturated fat: 7.1 g

Cholesterol: 74 mg
Carbohydrates: 40.7 g
Protein: 32.2 g
Sodium: 883 mg

~ Chiles Stuffed with Mushrooms and Spinach

Yield: 6 servings

Mornings in Mexico are often filled with the pleasant aroma of roasted chiles as cooks in restaurants throughout the country rise early to begin preparing this common afternoon entrée.

Ingredients for the Chiles

6 large *chiles poblanos*
6 oz (175 g) Monterey Jack cheese, cut in ⅛-inch wide (0.3-cm) slices
6 oz (175 g) mushrooms, chopped
3 cups (750 ml) chopped fresh spinach

Ingredients for the Sauce

2 teaspoons corn oil
2 slices white onion, ¼-inch (0.5-cm) thick each
1 clove garlic
5 large roma tomatoes or 2 large regular tomatoes, quartered
2½ cups (560 ml) water
Salt and pepper, to taste

Preparation

Roast and peel the chiles as described on page 19. Slit each chile down one side, not quite all the way. Remove the seeds and veins. Set aside one-third of the cheese slices for later. Stuff each chile with one or two of the remaining cheese slices, some mushroom, and some spinach. Pinch the opening of each chile and pierce the flesh with a toothpick to close the gap: "over-under-over," as you would a safety pin. Set the stuffed chiles aside.

To prepare the sauce, heat the oil in a deep frying pan or sauté pan over medium heat. Add one onion slice and blacken. Put the remaining onion slice, garlic, tomatoes, and 1½ cups (375 ml) water in blender and purée. Add the purée to the pan with the blackened onion and simmer for 5 minutes. Add 1 cup (250 ml) water, season with salt and pepper, and simmer for 5 minutes.

Put the stuffed chiles in the pan with the sauce. Cover, turn the heat to low, and cook for 10 minutes. Remove the lid, lay the remaining cheese slices on the chiles, cover, and cook for 5 minutes. Serve, accompanied by warm corn tortillas. (Don't forget to remove the toothpicks before you eat the chiles.)

∾ South of the Border

Fans of stuffed chiles should also check out *Chiles Rellenos de Arroz Integral* (pages 110–111) and *Ensalada de Chiles Rellenos* (pages 154–155).

Nutrition Information
Amounts per Serving (including three corn tortillas)

Calories: 343
Calories from fat: 31.1%
Total fat: 12.3 g
Saturated fat: 5.9 g

Cholesterol: 25 mg
Carbohydrates:47.0 g
Protein: 14.5 g
Sodium: 664 mg

∾ Flautas

Yield: 4 servings

Literally "flutes," these thin and crispy treats are wonderful as hors d'oeuvres, a quick appetizer, or a light meal.

Ingredients

2 cups (500 ml) chopped or shredded green cabbage
2 cups (500 ml) chopped green leaf lettuce
1 medium tomato, seeded and chopped
Juice of 1–2 limes
3 large split chicken breasts
15 white corn tortillas, 5 inches (12.5 cm) in diameter

Preparation

Mix cabbage, lettuce, tomato, and lime juice in a bowl and put in the refrigerator. Poach and shred the chicken as described on page 19. Put the shredded chicken in a bowl and mix well with the salsa.

Lower the broiling rack to its lowest setting, and preheat the broiler. Roll tortillas as for enchiladas (page 49), filling them with about 3 tablespoons of the chicken mixture; for *flautas,* roll the tortillas tighter and smaller than for enchiladas, ¾–1 inch (2–2.5 cm) in diameter. Fill the baking dish with the *flautas,* then coat them with cooking spray.

Broil the *flautas* for 5–7 minutes until they are toasted brown and crispy. Remove them from the broiler, top the individual servings with the lettuce and cabbage mixture, and serve, accompanied by your favorite salsa.

Variations

Mix shredded low-fat mozzarella or cheddar cheese into the chicken filling before rolling the flautas.

Nutrition Information
Amounts per Serving

Calories: 359	Cholesterol: 61 mg
Calories from fat: 9.3%	Carbohydrates: 57.8 g
Total fat: 3.8 g	Protein: 31.0 g
Saturated fat: 0.7 g	Sodium: 336 mg

❧ *Carne Guisada*
Mexican-Style Stewed Beef

Yield: 4 servings

Cooked along both sides of the border, *Carne Guisada* is a staple beef dish of Mexican cooking. This is a modified version of a recipe given to me by Eva Infante of San Antonio, Texas. Serve it with beans, rice, and tortillas for a classic *Tejano* meal.

Ingredients

1 ½ pounds (¾ kg) top round steak or other lean beef
1 small white onion, chopped
2 cloves garlic, finely chopped
1 can stewed tomatoes, 14 oz (392 g)
1 ½ cup (375 ml) water
1 teaspoon ground toasted cumin seed or powdered cumin
1 ½ tablespoons sifted flour
Salt and pepper, to taste (optional)

Preparation

Trim the meat of all visible fat, then cut into bite-size cubes. Heat a large nonstick sauté pan or Dutch oven over medium heat. Add the meat and brown for 3–5 minutes. Remove the meat and set aside. Add the onion and garlic to the pan and sauté for 3 minutes in the fat exuded by the meat. Add tomatoes, stir, and simmer for 2 minutes.

Add the water and cumin to pan. Return the beef to the pan, stir, and bring to a boil. Reduce the heat to low, cover, and simmer about 1 hour until the meat is tender.

While the meat is cooking, heat a nonstick frying pan over medium-high heat. Add flour and toast for 4 minutes until brown. When the meat is tender, remove cover and gradually stir in flour. Cover the pan and simmer gently for 5–10 minutes, stirring occasionally, until any taste of raw flour is gone. Season with salt and pepper, and serve.

Nutrition Information
Amounts per Serving

Calories: 268	Cholesterol: 88 mg
Calories from fat: 26.4%	Carbohydrates: 13.3 g
Total fat: 7.8 g	Protein: 35.4 g
Saturated fat: 2.6 g	Sodium: 619 mg

Part II

La Comida de Mexico
Traditional Mexican Cuisine

From rural villages to crowded cities, meal preparation in Mexico starts with a trip to the local market, or *el mercado*. There, amongst a labyrinth of goods ranging from flowers to pots to pigs passing through the hands of a constant flux of humanity, exists a mind-boggling collection of fresh and colorful foodstuffs. Ripe tomatoes, tomatillos, chiles, mangoes, and avocados; freshly made cheese, tamales, and tortillas; and cut-to-order meats and seafood are just some of the items to be purchased and carried home for immediate use. More exotic products, such as *flor de calabaza* (squash flower), *huitlacoche* (corn fungus), and *chapulines* (dried grasshoppers), are also available, depending on the area. It is this freshness and regionalism of ingredients that perhaps best characterizes Mexican cuisine.

At the same time, the life of the Mexican cook has been touched by modernization. Even in smaller towns, *supermercados* (supermarkets ranging in size from our gas-pump mini-marts to umpteen-aisle warehouses) are commonplace. Milk, butter, and other disposable goods, as well as canned tomatoes, breakfast cereals, soda, and so on, can be purchased at these increasingly popular convenience stores. In turn, Mexicans have had their effect on the supermarket ideal. Tubs of *mole* pastes, *arroz a la Mexicana*, and pickled vegetable dishes known as *escabeches* are among the homemade creations available at the modern Mexican *super*.

Through the tradition of their vivacious *mercados* and the practicality of the newfound *supermercados*, Mexicans continue to develop one of the finest styles of cooking in the world. Unfortunately, the truth is that they do tend to cook with a large amount of lard and oil. In the following pages you will discover lighter versions of dishes as they are prepared in Mexico today. Who knows, with the growing worldwide concern for nutrition, you may be enjoying the Mexican cuisine of tomorrow.

Chapter 3

Salsas y Mas
Hot Sauces and More

Much of the color, flavor, and life of traditional Mexican cuisine comes from distinctive condiments used to enhance prepared dishes. Simple garnishes, such as lime wedges, chopped cilantro, chile, cabbage, or onion, as well as more elaborate pickled vegetables and salsas, cooperate to give the Mexican table its festive character. Broiled and roasted meats, chicken, fish, eggs, soups, beans, and even plain boiled rice easily become a healthy Mexican meal when served with some warm corn tortillas and a few of these delicious accouterments.

The best-known Mexican condiment in the United States is table salsa, known south of the border as *salsa cruda* or *salsa de molcajete*. (A *salsa cocida*, on the other hand, is a cooked sauce that is part of a particular dish, like a spaghetti sauce.) Table salsas are loaded with vitamins and minerals; they contain virtually no fat and almost always include fresh, dried, or smoked chiles. In the United States these salsas are frequently used as a tasty dip for tortilla chips or vegetables, but not so in Mexico, where they are simply spooned over dishes to add texture and piquancy.

In any case, learning to make a good table salsa is the starting point of low-fat Mexican cooking. Begin by using the freshest ingredients available (canned tomatoes can be substituted, but avoid canned tomatillos), and remember that texture is paramount to the quality of a salsa. In general, chop ingredients by hand and use the blender merely to mix everything together; do not purée ingredients, as this robs a sauce of its character. And, keep in mind that many salsas taste better if they've been allowed to season for 30 minutes to 1 hour, although a few, such as *Salsa Mexicana*, are best eaten immediately.

The following salsas and relishes represent some of the splendid flavors, aromas, and colors found on the Mexican table. Use them to add extra flavor not just to the dishes in this book, but to any food that needs a little zip.

∿ Salsa Mexicana (Pico de Gallo) Classic Mexican Table Salsa

Yield: 1 ½ cups (375 ml)

This tried-and-true salsa, known as *Pico de Gallo* in the United States, can be found on just about every luncheonette table in Mexico, usually next to a bowl of *Salsa Verde* (page 71). It is an excellent dip for baked tortilla chips and superb on eggs, tacos, burritos, beans, baked potatoes, rice— just about anything.

Ingredients

2 medium ripe tomatoes, seeded
½ large white onion
1–3 *chiles serranos*
½ teaspoon salt
⅓ cup (80 ml) cold water or lime juice
½ cup (125 ml) chopped cilantro

Preparation

Finely chop the tomatoes, onion, and *chiles serranos,* and put them in a nonmetallic bowl. Add salt and water or lime juice and mix everything well. Allow flavors to blend for 5 minutes, then add the cilantro, and mix well. Wait 5 minutes and serve.

Variations

Substitute fresh oregano for the cilantro and you have *Salsa Fresca,* another common Mexican table salsa.

∿ Tips

Salsa Mexicana is best served freshly made. It will not keep at all.

Nutrition Information
Serving: ½ cup (125 ml)
Amounts per Serving

Calories: 83	Cholesterol: 0 mg
Calories from fat: 5.1%	Carbohydrates: 19.2 g
Total fat: 0.6 g	Protein: 4.0 g
Saturated fat: 0.0 g	Sodium: 472 mg

∾ Salsa Verde
Tomatillo-Cilantro Green Sauce

Yield: 2 cups (500 ml)

This classic salsa is found everywhere south of the border, from humble homes to upscale eateries. In fact, it is probably the most popular condiment in Mexico. Spoon it on fish, meats, eggs, *quesadillas*, and vegetables, or use it as a chip dip.

Ingredients

8 medium tomatillos (¾ pounds or 300 g)
1–3 *chiles serranos*, finely chopped
1 clove garlic, chopped
¼ medium white onion, roughly chopped
½ cup (125 ml) chopped cilantro
½ teaspoon salt

Preparation

Remove the husks and stems from the tomatillos. Put the tomatillos in a saucepan, cover with water, and bring to a boil. Simmer gently for 8–10 minutes until the tomatillos are soft. Remove the pan from the heat and allow the tomatillos to cool in the cooking water. Put the chiles, garlic, onion, cilantro, salt, and ½ cup (125 ml) of the cooking water in a blender and purée. Transfer the tomatillos to the blender using a slotted spoon. Purée and serve.

Variations

Serve sprinkled with a teaspoon or two of chopped cilantro atop the *Salsa Verde* for a true Mexican touch.

For a popular Mexican variation, boil and purée 1–3 *chiles de árbol* with the tomatillos.

∾ Tips

This sauce will keep in the refrigerator for about a week but the tomatillos' consistency may cause it to thicken. In this case, heat the salsa until the desired consistency is attained; then cool to room temperature and serve.

Nutrition Information

Serving: ½ cup (125 ml)

Amounts per Serving

Calories: 51   Cholesterol: 0 mg
Calories from fat: 7.8%   Carbohydrates: 10.2 g
Total fat: 0.5 g   Protein: 2.3 g
Saturated fat: 0.0 g   Sodium: 327 mg

ꙮ Salsa Casera
Roasted Tomato Salsa

Yield: 1 ¼ cups (300 ml)

A request for salsa in Mexico usually gets you *Salsa Verde* (page 71), *Salsa Mexicana* (page 70), or a dried chile purée salsa. If you're looking for something similar to the tomato salsas common in the United States, ask for *Salsa Casera*, which literally means "homestyle sauce."

Ingredients

3 medium ripe tomatoes (1 pound or ½ kg)
½ clove garlic, finely chopped
½ teaspoon salt
1 large *chile serrano*, finely chopped
¼ cup (60 ml) finely chopped white onion
Pinch of sugar
Freshly ground black pepper (optional)

Preparation

Broil tomatoes as described on pages 18–19 and allow them to cool. Put the garlic and salt in a blender. Add the smallest tomato, unpeeled, and purée. Peel and seed the remaining two tomatoes, transfer them to a bowl, and chop finely. Pour the contents of the blender into a separate nonmetallic bowl. Add chopped tomatoes and mix. Add chile, onion, sugar, and pepper. Mix well and chill in the refrigerator for 30 minutes before serving.

ꙮ Tips

The quality of this salsa depends on the tomatoes, so use homegrown if possible.

For a thicker salsa, seed the smallest tomato as well, but do not discard the skin, as this adds to the flavor and presentation.

Nutrition Information
Serving: ½ cup (125 ml)
Amounts per Serving

Calories: 49	Cholesterol: 0 mg
Calories from fat: 3.5%	Carbohydrates: 11.1 g
Total fat: 0.2 g	Protein: 2.1 g
Saturated fat: 0.0 g	Sodium: 301 mg

∾ Salsa de Jitomate y Chile Chipotle
Tomato and Chile Chipotle Salsa

Yield: 2 cups (500 ml)

The *chile chipotle*, or smoked *jalapeño*, continues to grow in popularity in the United States, as more restaurant menus introduce dishes containing the fiery pepper. The heat of this tasty salsa, which works as a dip or condiment, can be controlled by adding more or fewer chiles and accompanying *adobo* sauce.

Ingredients

½ clove garlic, minced
2 tablespoons finely chopped white onion
2 tablespoons chopped scallion greens
1 can stewed tomatoes, 14 oz (392 g), or 3 ripe medium tomatoes,
    broiled, peeled, seeded, and chopped
½ teaspoon salt
1–3 canned *chiles chipotles* in *adobo* sauce

Preparation

Put the garlic, onion, scallion greens, tomatoes, and salt in a blender. Add the *chile chipotles* plus some *adobo* sauce and pulse-blend coarsely. Do not purée as the sauce should be thick with plenty of texture. Pour the contents of the blender into a bowl or glass jar with a lid and chill in the refrigerator for at least 15 minutes. Serve.

∾ Tips

This salsa can be stored in a covered glass jar in the refrigerator for up to two weeks.

Nutrition Information
Serving: ½ cup (125 ml)
Amounts per Serving

Calories: 37
Calories from fat: 4.0%
Total fat: 0.2 g
Saturated fat: 0 g

Cholesterol: 0 mg
Carbohydrates: 9.1 g
Protein: 1.5 g
Sodium: 450 mg

◌ Salsa Linda/Pretty Salsa

Yield: About 2 cups

This sauce highlights the distinctive color and flavor of the one and only *chile habanero*. Popular in Yucatán under the Mayan name *Salsa X-Ni-Pek*, it is *muy picosa* (HOT!) and looks almost too good to eat. But don't let this stop you from enjoying it as a refreshing all-purpose condiment or dip for baked tortilla chips.

Ingredients

2 large ripe tomatoes, seeded and chopped
½ large purple onion, chopped
1 *chile habanero*, chopped
Juice of ½ medium orange
Juice of 1 lime
Juice of 1 lemon
½ cup (125 ml) chopped cilantro
½ teaspoon salt

Preparation

Mix the tomatoes, onion, and chile in a nonmetallic bowl. Mix the citrus juices together and add them to the bowl. Mix and allow flavors to blend for 5 minutes. Add the cilantro and salt, and mix well. Refrigerate for 10 minutes before serving.

◌ Tips

This salsa is best served freshly made. It will not keep at all.

Substitute 3 *chiles serranos* if *chile habanero* is unavailable.

Nutrition Information
Serving: ½ cup (125 ml)
Amounts per Serving

Calories: 76
Calories from fat: 5.0%
Total fat: 0.5 g
Saturated fat: 0 g

Cholesterol: 0 mg
Carbohydrates: 19.7 g
Protein: 3.6 g
Sodium: 288 mg

❦ *Salsa de Chile de Árbol*
Smoky Dried Chile Salsa

Yield: About 2 cups (500 ml)

The smoky flavor and unique color of this super-hot salsa make it a nice alternative to the standard green or red sauce. In addition to being a fiery chip dip, it is fantastic on chicken, beans, and eggs. A few bites will also supply you with a full day's requirement of vitamin C.

Ingredients

1 teaspoon corn oil
10–20 *chiles de árbol*
2 small cloves garlic, minced
⅓ cup (80 ml) finely chopped white onion
½ teaspoon salt
½ cup (125 ml) water
2 large roma tomatoes, peeled, seeded, and roughly chopped
2 medium tomatillos, roughly chopped

Preparation

Heat the oil in a frying pan over medium heat. Add the chiles and cook until browned and fragrant. Remove the chiles and set aside on a plate lined with paper toweling. Put the garlic, onion, salt, and water in a blender. Remove stems from chiles. Add the chiles to the blender and blend everything for about 30 seconds until well ground.

Add tomatoes and tomatillos to the blender and pulse-blend, retaining a good texture to the sauce. Pour the contents of the blender into a nonmetallic bowl or glass jar with a lid and chill in the refrigerator for at least 1 hour before serving.

❦ Tips

This salsa will keep in a covered glass jar in the refrigerator for about ten days.

Nutrition Information
Serving: ½ cup (125 ml)
Amounts per Serving

Calories: 127
Calories from fat: 10.7%
Total fat: 1.7 g
Saturated fat: 0.2 g

Cholesterol: 0 mg
Carbohydrates: 26.9 g
Protein: 5.5 g
Sodium: 406 mg

❧ *Salsa de Chile en Polvo*
Ground Chile Salsa

Yield: About 2 cups (500 ml)

This earthy salsa is scrumptious over broiled chicken or beef and white rice.

Ingredients

4 *chiles guajillos, pasillas,* or New Mexican dried red chile
1 clove garlic, minced
1 slice white onion, $\frac{1}{4}$-inch thick (0.5-cm)
1 large ripe tomato, broiled and peeled, or 1 can whole tomatoes,
    14.5 oz (406 g), drained
$\frac{1}{4}$ teaspoon salt, or to taste
Pinch of ground toasted cumin seed or powdered cumin
Pinch of sugar

Preparation

Wipe the chiles clean with a damp towel. Put the chiles in a cast-iron or nonstick frying pan and toast over medium-high heat for 4–6 minutes until dark and aromatic; press with a spatula while toasting. Remove the chiles from the heat, let cool, and crumble into a spice grinder or mortar. Grind the chiles and set aside.

Put the garlic, onion, and tomatoes in a blender and pulse-blend. Transfer to a nonmetallic bowl; add salt, cumin, and sugar; and mix well. Stir in ground chile, then let salsa chill in refrigerator for 1–2 hours before serving.

❧ Tips

Be careful not to blister the skins of the chiles when toasting; this will impart a bitter taste to the salsa.

Nutrition Information
Serving: ½ cup (125 ml)
Amounts per Serving

Calories: 39	Cholesterol: 0 mg
Calories from fat: 3.7%	Carbohydrates: 8.8 g
Total fat: 0.2 g	Protein: 1.8 g
Saturated fat: 0.0 g	Sodium: 278 mg

✒ Salsa Suave/Cool Hot Sauce

Yield: About 2 cups (500 ml)

I saw this salsa being made in the central market of Cuernavaca, and asked *la señora* preparing it if she had forgotten to add chile. She explained, *"No tiene chile, joven, es suave."*("It doesn't contain chile, young man, it's mild.") Perfect for people who prefer a cool hot sauce, *Salsa Suave* is great on tacos, rice, beans, and eggs, served warm (especially) or cold.

Ingredients

1 clove garlic, minced
⅓ cup (80 ml) finely chopped white onion
¼ teaspoon salt
3 medium ripe tomatoes (1 pound or ½ kg), broiled and peeled, or 1 can whole tomatoes, 14.5 oz (406 g), drained (reserve juice)
1 teaspoon corn or olive oil
¼ teaspoon ground toasted oregano
Pinch of black pepper (optional)

Preparation

Put the garlic, onion, salt, and ½ cup (125 ml) water or reserved tomato juice in a blender and blend until smooth. Add tomatoes and purée. Heat the oil in a frying pan over medium heat. Add the contents of blender to the pan and stir immediately. Add oregano and pepper, stir, and cook the sauce for 4–6 minutes until it has thickened, stirring frequently. Remove the pan from the heat and allow the sauce to cool for 2 minutes. Serve warm in a nonmetallic bowl or chill in the refrigerator for 2 hours before serving.

Variations

For a rich, flavorful twist, use ½ cup (125 ml) clear chicken broth in place of the water or reserved tomato juice.

Nutrition Information
Serving: ½ cup (125 ml)
Amounts per Serving

Calories: 33
Calories from fat: 31.4%
Total fat: 1.2 g
Saturated fat: 0.2 g

Cholesterol: 0 mg
Carbohydrates: 5.1 g
Protein: 0.9 g
Sodium: 191 mg

❧ Salsa Macha/Macho Sauce

Yield: 1 cup (250 ml)

This blazing salsa is one of my favorites. The fiery pulp of the *chile jalapeño* and the unique flavor of the cilantro create a perfect condiment for eggs, tacos, beans, and meats. Fair warning: This salsa is not for the lily-tongued.

Ingredients

8 *chiles jalapeños*
1 cup chopped cilantro
1 clove garlic
½ cup (125 ml) water
¼ teaspoon salt

Preparation

Roast the chiles as described on page 19, peel, and remove stems. Put chiles in a blender, add the remaining ingredients, and blend until smooth. Refrigerate for at least 30 minutes before serving. Use sparingly.

Variations

Chiles serranos are an acceptable substitute for the *chiles jalapeños*, but watch out for the additional heat.

❧ Tips

This salsa can be stored in a covered glass jar in the refrigerator for up to three weeks. If the salsa is too thick, thin it with a little water or lime juice.

Nutrition Information
Serving: ¼ cup (60 ml)
Amounts per Serving

Calories: 57
Calories from fat: 7.1%
Total fat: 0.5 g
Saturated fat: 0 g

Cholesterol: 0 mg
Carbohydrates: 12.5 g
Protein: 3.4 g
Sodium: 156 mg

❧ *Salsa del Infierno*
"Hot as Hell" Salsa

Yield: About 1 cup (250 ml)

This salsa is based on a delicious but insanely hot sauce I experienced in Mérida, Yucatán. Upon sampling a bit of the normally all-chile salsa, I immediately started sweating in the 100°F (38°C) heat of the day, gulping soda, and imploring someone—anyone—to make the pain stop. This milder version is especially good on seafood and chicken, and is essential as an accompaniment to *Vuelve a la Vida* (pages 185–186) and Black Bean Tacos (pages 45–46).

Ingredients

1 small carrot
1–2 *chiles habaneros*
½ cup (125 ml) carrot juice
¼ cup (60 ml) finely chopped white onion
¼ teaspoon salt
2 teaspoons white vinegar
1 teaspoon fresh orange juice
Juice of 1 lime

Preparation

Put the carrot in a medium saucepan, cover with water, and simmer about 10 minutes until soft; let it cool in the cooking water. Remove stems from the chile(s). Roast the chile(s) in a hot skillet until charred on all sides. Drain the carrot and transfer to a blender. Add the chile, carrot juice, onion, salt, and vinegar, and purée. Add citrus juices and ¼ cup (60 ml) water and pulse-blend to mix. Pour the salsa into a nonmetallic bowl and chill in refrigerator for about 45 minutes before serving.

❧ Tips

Wash your hands immediately after you finish handling the *chile habanero*.

Nutrition Information
Serving: ½ cup (125 ml)
Amounts per Serving

Calories: 67	Cholesterol: 0 mg
Calories from fat: 3.4%	Carbohydrates: 17.0 g
Total fat: 0.3 g	Protein: 2.4 g
Saturated fat: 0 g	Sodium: 360 mg

∾ Jalapeños en Escabeche
Pickled Jalapeños with Onion and Carrots

Yield: 6 servings

This incomparable relish is wonderful with eggs, enchiladas, tacos, beans, and so on. If you want to impress a Mexican with your knowledge of Mexican cuisine as well as your advanced level of heat tolerance, ask for *Jalapeños en Escabeche* with your meal.

Ingredients

1 teaspoon olive oil
8–10 whole *chiles jalapeños*
1 large carrot, cut into thin ovals
½ medium white onion, sliced
4 cloves garlic
1 cup (250 ml) water
1 teaspoon dried oregano
¼ teaspoon dried thyme
¼ teaspoon dried marjoram
2 bay leaves
Black pepper, to taste
¼ cup (60 ml) wine vinegar
½ cup (125 ml) white vinegar
½ teaspoon salt

Preparation

Heat olive oil in a nonstick frying pan over medium heat. Add chiles, carrot, onion, and garlic, and stir-fry for 5 minutes. Add the water, cover, and simmer for 4 minutes.

Remove the lid from the pan, and add herbs, bay leaves, black pepper, wine vinegar, and ¼ cup (60 ml) of the white vinegar. Stir well, cover, and simmer gently for 5 minutes until the chiles are tender. Remove the pan from the heat, and allow the chiles to cool, covered, for 5 minutes.

Remove the lid, add salt, stir, and put everything, including any liquid, in a pint-sized glass jar. Add the remaining ¼ cup (60 ml) white vinegar and enough water to cover chiles. Cover the jar and refrigerate for at least 24 hours. Serve as a relish.

∾ Rajas/Strips of Roasted Green Chile and Onion

Yield: 1 ½ cups (375 ml)

Mild, sweet, and full of vitamins, these chile strips are wonderful on eggs, tacos, burritos, enchiladas, and meats, and in submarine and pita-bread sandwiches. Or, roll a spoonful in a warm corn or flour tortilla for a delicious snack.

Ingredients

4 large *chiles poblanos* or Anaheim peppers
1 teaspoon corn oil
1 small white onion, cut into thin strips
4 tablespoons water
Salt, to taste

Preparation

Roast and peel the chiles as described on page 19. Remove stems and seeds, and cut into ¼- to ½-inch (0.5- to 1.25-cm) strips. Heat the oil in a non-stick frying pan or sauté pan over medium heat. Add the onion and stir-fry for 3 minutes. Add 2 tablespoons water, stir, cover, and cook about 5 minutes until the onion is soft. Remove the lid, add chiles, and stir. Add 2 more tablespoons water, sprinkle with salt and cook about 2 minutes or until the water has evaporated. Serve as a relish.

Variations

Rajas Encurtidas: Pickle the onion and roasted *poblano* strips instead of sautéing them by putting them in a bowl with 1 cup (250 ml) fresh lime juice, ½ teaspoon toasted dried oregano, and salt. Marinate for 3–4 hours. Serve as a relish.

Nutrition Information
Servings: ½ cup (125 ml)
Amounts per Serving

Calories: 41
Calories from fat: 25.0%
Total fat: 1.3 g
Saturated fat:0.2 g

Cholesterol: 0 mg
Carbohydrates: 7.2 g
Protein: 1.5 g
Sodium: 141 mg

❧ Cebollas Desflameadas
Mild Crisped Onions

Yield: 6 servings

This recipe may seem silly, but try these water-crisped onions and you'll be amazed at the transformation the cold water brings. Gone is the dreaded sting of the white onion, leaving behind a sweet, crunchy garnish for topping chicken, enchiladas, *Enfrijoladas* (pages 194–195), *Chilaquiles* (pages 196–197), burritos, salads, sandwiches, beans, and so on.

Ingredients
1 medium white onion, thinly sliced

Preparation
Put the onion slices in a bowl and cover with plenty of cold water. Chill in the refrigerator for 30 minutes. Remove, drain slices, and separate into rings. Set rings on a plate lined with paper toweling for 5 minutes to dry. Pat dry, transfer to a bowl, and refrigerate until serving.

❧ Tips
Stored in a covered glass jar, these onions will keep indefinitely in the refrigerator.

Nutrition Information
Amounts per Serving

Calories: 5	Cholesterol: 0 mg
Calories from fat: 0%	Carbohydrates: 1.0 g
Total fat: 0 g	Protein: 0.2 g
Saturated fat: 0 g	Sodium: 0.2 mg

∾ Cebollas Encurtidas
Hot Pickled Onions

Yield: 6 servings

Ingredients

1 medium white onion, thinly sliced
1 *chile habanero*, seeded and cut into thin rings or strips
¼ teaspoon toasted dried oregano
1 clove garlic, mashed
3 peppercorns, crushed
1 bay leaf
1 cup (250 ml) white vinegar
½ cup (125 ml) water
½ teaspoon salt

Preparation

Put the onions in a bowl, cover with water, and soak for 10 minutes. Drain and put in a small bowl with the chile, oregano, garlic, peppercorns, and bay leaf. Mix vinegar and water together and pour over everything, add salt, and mix well. Transfer everything to a glass jar, cover, and chill in the refrigerator for at least two hours, preferably 1–2 days. Serve as a relish.

Nutrition Information
Amounts per Serving

Calories: 49
Calories from fat: 5.2%
Total fat: 0.4 g
Saturated fat: 0.1 g

Cholesterol: 0 mg
Carbohydrates: 12.9 g
Protein: 2.0 g
Sodium: 276 mg

∾ Cebollas a la Yucateca
Spiced Pickled Onions

Yield: About 2 cups (500 ml)

On Sundays in Mérida, Yucatán, food vendors fight for space in the town square to sell tamales, pork, and chicken cooked in banana leaves, as well as various turkey dishes. The standard relish for each of these inexpensive treats is these addictive onions, which are a tasty topping for submarine sandwiches as well.

Ingredients

1 large red onion, thinly sliced
½ cup (125 ml) white vinegar
½ teaspoon salt
Pinch of sugar
¼ teaspoon toasted dried oregano
3 peppercorns, crushed
3 whole cloves
2 allspice, crushed
2 cloves garlic, bruised

Preparation

Put the onion in a medium saucepan. Cover with boiling water and soak for 45 seconds; drain and return them to the saucepan. Mix the vinegar, salt, and sugar in a bowl; then add to the saucepan. Add the remaining ingredients, stir, and bring to a boil. Remove the pan from the heat, allow the contents to cool, and transfer them to a nonmetallic bowl. Cool, then serve as a relish.

∾ Tips

These onions will keep for 2–3 weeks stored in a covered glass jar in the refrigerator.

Nutrition Information
Serving: ½ cup (125 ml)
Amounts per Serving

Calories: 53
Calories from fat: 15.6%
Total fat: 1.2 g
Saturated fat: 0.3 g

Cholesterol: 0 mg
Carbohydrates: 12.8 g
Protein: 1.5 g
Sodium: 281 mg

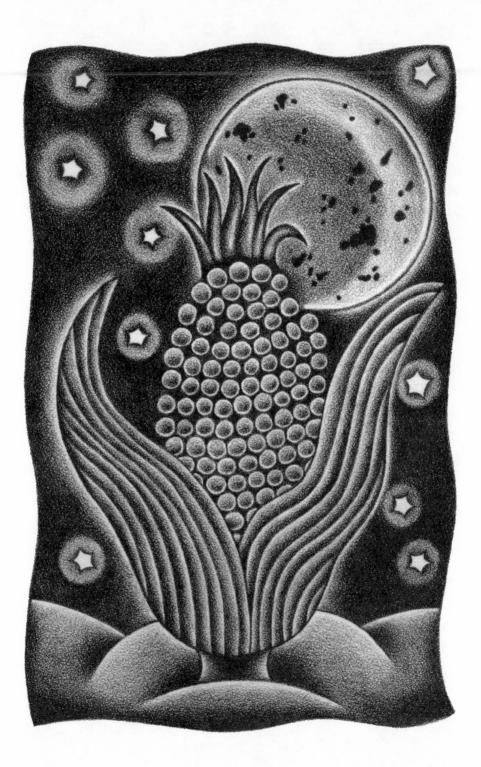

Chapter 4

La Tortilla de Maíz
The Corn Tortilla

Corn has long been one of Mexico's main sources of carbohydrates as well as a central part of its folklore. It was first cultivated in Mexico between 6,000 and 7,000 years ago, and some ancient natives even believed themselves to have been created by the gods out of the vaunted vegetable. Today, it is virtually impossible to find a *Mexicano* who does not adore this most essential of Mexican ingredients.

Most of the corn grown in Mexico is used to make tortillas— the "bread" of interior Mexican cuisine. Far superior to the commercial versions sold in the United States, Mexican corn tortillas are soft, doughy disks as flavorful as the finest wheat loaf. They are also quite versatile. A corn tortilla can be used to wrap a bit of food along with some salsa or chile for an instant taco, giving sustenance to the skimpiest of courses. Or, more commonly, it is rolled tightly and used as an edible utensil to push food onto a fork, scoop beans, or sop up a sauce. In any case, with its ability to turn scraps into a feast and its time-tested nutritive value, the corn tortilla is the staff of Mexican life.

Flour tortillas, which are more prominent in American-Mexican fare than their corn counterparts, are actually a relatively recent creation. Invented after the Spanish brought wheat to the New World, they are common only in northern Mexico and the United States, remaining more or less a curiosity in the majority of the Mexican cooking world.

✍ The Lowfat Lifesaver

The corn tortilla also plays a central role in low-fat Mexican cuisine. It is low in calories (60) and extremely low in fat (about 0.5 g, no saturated fat) and percentage of total calories from fat (10 percent). In fact, 80 percent of its calories are in the form of carbohydrates, the base of the USDA Food Pyramid. Thus, eating a few corn tortillas with a meal is a great way to reduce the percentage of the meal's fat calories without an excessive increase in the meal's total number of calories.

A flour tortilla, on the other hand, contains about two-and-a-half times as much fat as a corn tortilla (including 1 g of saturated fat) and almost twice as many calories—not quite the meal saver that its corn cousin is.

∿ Making the Perfect Tortilla

Yield: About 18 tortillas, 5 inches (12.5 cm) in diameter

Although commercial corn tortillas are certainly convenient, *tortillas a mano*, or handmade tortillas, are well worth the effort if you have the time. Although you may be intimidated by the prospect of creating your own tortillas, after a few attempts and accepting that not all tortillas turn out, you will soon be surprising yourself and impressing your guests with delicious authentic corn wraps.

As most people do not have half an afternoon to pat out tortillas by hand, investing in a tortilla press is a good idea. Most Mexican markets in the United States and many houseware departments carry tortilla presses. Buy one that is at least 6 inches (15 cm) in diameter. In general, the heavier presses work the best.

Ingredients
3 cups (750 ml) or 1 pound ($\frac{1}{2}$ kg) corn flour (*masa harina*)
1 $\frac{1}{2}$–2 cups (375–500 ml) water

Preparing the *Masa* (Tortilla Dough)
Put the corn flour in a large bowl. Add 1 $\frac{1}{2}$ cups (375 ml) water and mix well; form into a large ball. The resulting dough, or *masa*, should be smooth and feel like an earlobe. If it is cracking or crumbly, it is too dry; add the remaining water and knead well. If it sticks to your hand, it is too wet; add a bit more flour until it is soft and smooth. When the *masa* is ready, store it in a large plastic bag to keep it from drying out as you proceed. If it dehydrates, moisten it by working in a few drops of water.

Pressing the *Masa*
You will need a plastic bag (the quart or liter size is good) or a plastic produce bag from the supermarket. Cut the bag in half (cut off the plastic zipper if there is one); then cut each half into a square approximately 6 inches by 6 inches (15 cm by 15 cm). Open the tortilla press and center one plastic square on the bottom face of the press. Set the other square aside.

Pinch a small portion of *masa* and form it into a ball 1 $\frac{1}{2}$ inches (3.75 cm) in diameter. Place the ball on the plastic square on the tortilla press, slightly off-center towards the press's hinge. (You don't want to place the ball at the exact center of the press because as you squeeze the press, the *masa* is pushed away from the hinge and may spread out over the edge opposite the hinge.) Place the other plastic square on top of the ball and close the press firmly, but not so hard that the tortilla spreads out beyond the faces of the tortilla press. It should be all one motion. Lift off the top face of the press.

Heating the Tortilla

You're now ready to peel the tortilla from the plastic and heat it. First, heat a cast-iron or nonstick frying pan or a griddle over medium heat for 5 minutes until it reaches a constant temperature. Then, peel the tortilla from the plastic as follows: Pick up the plastic/tortilla/plastic "sandwich" and turn it over so that the bottom square is now on top; lay this flat in one hand. Then, using the other hand, slowly peel the plastic away from the tortilla, finding the best place to start peeling as you would with a sticker. When the bottom square is removed, flip the tortilla/plastic over so that the plastic is on top, and repeat the peeling process just described. Always peel the plastic, not the tortilla.

Rearrange the peeled tortilla so that it rests in both hands (do not flip!) and lay it as flatly as possible in the bottom of the frying pan. If the pan is hot enough and the dough is sufficiently moist, steam will come out from underneath the tortilla in about 10 seconds. After 20–25 seconds, the edges of the tortilla should start to dry and the dough on the bottom side will have darkened a bit, with a speckled texture and perhaps a few light brown spots. This is the sign to flip the tortilla, either by hand or using a spatula.

Ideally, the tortilla should not bubble anywhere once it is flipped (though it is OK if it bubbles a little at the edges; if it bubbles on its inner part, the heat is too high). Heat the tortilla for 40–50 seconds until the facedown side is speckled with brown spots. Next, turn the tortilla over one last time. It should puff up full of steam into what looks like a miniature pillow, which means the tortilla will be fully cooked—light and perfect. If it doesn't puff up right away, try assisting it by "tickling" it, pressing down on the tortilla with your fingers for an instant. Don't be discouraged if it doesn't work; not all tortillas pan out. After about 30 seconds, the tortilla is ready. Remove it and store it wrapped in a dry dishtowel, in a tortilla warmer, or in a sealed zipper-lock bag. Repeat these steps until all the *masa* is used up, stacking the tortillas made inside the towel, tortilla warmer, or plastic bag.

Variations

Although tortillas are by far the most popular form of processed corn flour, Mexicans have developed many other variations of *masa*; an approximately analogous situation would be spaghetti, which is a popular pasta form among many different cultures, with varying shapes, sizes, and textures. Other *masa* recipes in this book are *Sopes* (pages 202–203) and *Quesadillas Estilo Mexico* (pages 183–184).

Chapter 5

Platos Fuertes
Main Dishes

Each afternoon in Mexico from about 2:00 to 4:00, families gather in their homes for the midday respite known as *siesta*. Shops close, market crowds thin, and neighborhoods grow quiet. And before they rest a bit prior to returning to work—which often lasts until 8:00 or 9:00 P.M.—Mexicans take time to eat their main meal of the day, *comida corrida*.

This daily feast typically consists of soup, rice, or both; a main course; beans; tortillas; possibly another side dish; and dessert. And although the beans are always satisfying and the soup often splendid, for me the highlight of *comida corrida* is invariably the entree.

Mexican main courses usually consist of chicken, beef, or seafood in a flavorful but surprisingly mild sauce (vegetarian dishes are rare, except for cheese-stuffed *chiles rellenos*). These unassuming preparations roar to life, however, when complemented with a salsa or relish and a tortilla or two.

Most of the following dishes will serve six people as part of a multicourse meal, but each will also make a simple light dinner for three or four persons, served merely with a few warm tortillas, condiments, and perhaps a smattering of rice or refried beans.

¡A salud!

❧ Picadillo/Mexican Minced Meat

Yield: 6 servings

Every cook in Mexico seems to have her or his own version of this culinary collage. This recipe is a combination of various renditions I tasted while south of the border. *Picadillo* is most frequently served with tortillas as tacos, but it can also be used as filling for *chiles rellenos*, as an appetizer, *botana* (snack), and so on.

Ingredients

1 tablespoon olive oil
2 pounds (1 kg) extra-lean ground turkey
2 cloves garlic, minced
1 large white onion, chopped
2 tablespoons water
2 medium ripe tomatoes, chopped
⅓ cup (80 ml) chopped fresh Italian parsley
8 large stuffed green olives, sliced
¼ cup (60 ml) raisins
⅛ teaspoon ground cinnamon
Pinch of ground clove
Pinch of ground toasted cumin seed or powdered cumin
½ teaspoon salt
¼ cup (60 ml) slivered toasted almonds
1 medium russet potato, peeled, boiled, and diced

Preparation

Heat the oil in a large nonstick or cast-iron frying pan over medium-low heat. Add the turkey, garlic, and onion. Stirring frequently, cook until most of turkey is white. Add the water and heat over medium heat for 10–12 minutes until the onion is soft. In a cast-iron skillet, toast the almonds until brown. Add almonds and all remaining ingredients except potato to turkey mixture; stir and simmer for 5 minutes, stirring frequently. Add the potato, stir, and simmer over medium-high heat for 10–12 minutes until most of the liquid in the pan is gone. Serve with rice and warm tortillas.

Nutrition Information
Amounts per Serving

Calories: 383
Calories from fat: 21.4%
Total fat: 9.4 g
Saturated fat: 1.6 g

Cholesterol: 73 mg
Carbohydrates: 36.3 g
Protein: 41.4 g
Sodium: 509 mg

❧ Mole con Pollo/Chicken in Chile-Chocolate-Nut Sauce

Yield: 6 servings

To me, *Mole Poblano* is the pinnacle of Mexican cooking. Created in a Conquest-era monastery of Puebla, the complex sauce is delectable over chicken enchiladas, eggs, and especially rice. *¡Qué rico!*

Ingredients

1½ tablespoons sesame seeds
3 tablespoons sliced almonds
⅓ cup (80 ml) chopped white onion
2 cloves garlic, minced
2 tablespoons reduced-fat peanut butter
1 slice wheat bread, toasted and crumbled
4 cups (1,000 ml) water
1½ teaspoons corn oil
6 *chiles anchos*
6 *chiles pasillas*
6 *chiles guajillos*
1 chicken bouillon cube
1–2 tablets, 2 oz (56 g) each, Mexican chocolate (Ibarra or other brand), broken into pieces
6 boneless, skinless chicken breasts
1 lime, quartered

Preparation

In a cast-iron skillet, toast the sesame seeds and almonds until brown. Transfer them to a blender; add the onion, garlic, peanut butter, toast, and 2 cups (500 ml) water. Blend until smooth. Heat the oil in a large saucepan over medium-low heat. Add the contents of the blender and simmer gently for 10–12 minutes until thick, stirring occasionally.

Meanwhile, clean and toast *chiles anchos* as described on pages 19–20. Do not soak. Put intact *chiles pasillas* and *guajillos* in a large cast-iron frying pan and heat over medium heat for 4–6 minutes. Turn the chiles frequently while toasting, pressing each with a spatula. Do not blister the skins, or chiles will taste bitter. When they are dark and aromatic, remove the chiles from the pan and allow them to cool. Remove and discard stems.

Preheat oven to 400°F (205°C). Tear three of each type of chile into pieces and transfer them (with seeds) to a blender. Add the bouillon cube and 1 cup (250 ml) water, and purée. Add purée to the saucepan with peanut mixture and stir well. Tear remaining chiles into pieces, put in the blender with 1 cup (250 ml) water, purée, and add to the saucepan as well. Bring the sauce to a boil, stirring continuously. Add 1 cup (250 ml) water and chocolate (1–2 tablets, depending on how sweet you want your *mole*). Bring to a boil; then simmer for 20–30 minutes over low heat, stirring occasionally, until fairly thick.

Meanwhile, rinse the chicken with water and pat dry. Rub with lime, then transfer to a large baking dish sprayed lightly with cooking spray. Bake for 10 minutes, turn pieces over, and continue to bake about 10 minutes more until cooked but still moist. Remove the chicken from the oven and place one breast on each of six plates. Smother with plenty of *mole* and serve, accompanied by warm corn tortillas.

∾ Tips

Mexican chocolate is an essential ingredient for this recipe. I found it impossible to create an authentic-tasting dish using any other kinds of chocolate, including cocoa powder and semi-sweet chocolate.

Nutrition Information
Amounts per Serving (with 2 corn tortillas)

Calories: 361
Calories from fat: 26.2%
Total fat: 10.4 g
Saturated fat: 1.6 g

Cholesterol: 51 mg
Carbohydrates: 38.6 g
Protein: 27.7 g
Sodium: 401 mg

∿ Tinga de Pollo
Chipotle Chicken Stew

Yield: 4–6 servings

Marked by a combination of Mexican *and* European preparation methods and ingredients, Pueblan dishes such as this one are regarded as some of the best in Mexico.

Ingredients

3 large split chicken breasts
1 tablespoon olive oil
1 medium white onion, chopped
2 cloves garlic, finely chopped
8 oz (225 g) raw *chorizo* (page 21) or commercial turkey *chorizo*
1 can crushed tomatoes, 14.5 oz (406 g)
2 canned *chiles chipotles* in *adobo*, chopped
Pinch of sugar
½ cup (125 ml) water
Salt and pepper, to taste
1 large potato, peeled, boiled, and cubed

Preparation

Poach the chicken as described on page 19, but tear the meat into bite-size pieces instead of shredding it; then set it aside. Heat oil in a small saucepan over medium-low heat. Add chopped onion and garlic, and sauté for 2–3 minutes. Add *chorizo* and sauté mixture for 4–6 minutes until the onion is soft.

Add the tomatoes, chiles (with a bit of *adobo* sauce), sugar, and water to the pan. Stir, season with salt and pepper, and add potatoes. Simmer for 20 minutes, stirring occasionally; then add the chicken and simmer until the contents have the consistency of a thick stew. Serve as tacos with corn tortillas and white rice.

Variations

Add more sugar, chile, and *adobo* sauce for *Turbo Tinga*.

∿Tips

If you don't feel like making *chorizo* and you can't find a turkey version, substitute 8 oz (224 g) extra-lean ground turkey and brown with 1 teaspoon chili powder.

Nutrition Information
Amounts per Serving

Calories: 224
Calories from fat: 23.1%
Total fat: 5.7 g
Saturated fat: 1.1 g

Cholesterol: 84 mg
Carbohydrates: 12.3 g
Protein: 30.4 g
Sodium: 489 mg

❧ *Arroz con Pollo*
Chicken with Rice

Yield: 4–6 servings

This dish is straight-up, south-of-the-border soul food, perfect for the family or an informal dinner party. It goes well with beans, soup, or vegetables, and is heavenly when accompanied by some homemade corn tortillas.

Ingredients

3 large split chicken breasts
2 cloves garlic, finely chopped
½ medium white onion, chopped
1 tablespoon corn oil
1 large *chile jalapeño*, finely chopped
1 cup (250 ml) long-grain white rice
½ teaspoon crushed dried oregano leaves or 1½ tablespoons
    chopped fresh oregano
1 can whole tomatoes, 14 oz (392 g), drained and chopped
2 cups (500 ml) *Caldo de Pollo* (pages 160–161) or 1 can clear chicken
    broth, 14.5 oz (406 g)
1 teaspoon salt
1 cup frozen peas, thawed

Preparation

Poach the chicken as described on page 19. Cut into bite-size pieces. Heat the oil over medium heat in a large nonstick sauté pan or frying pan. Add the chopped garlic, onion, and chile, and sauté about 2 minutes until the onion is soft. Add rice and cook for 3 minutes, stirring frequently. Add oregano and tomatoes, stir, and heat through.

Add broth, 1 teaspoon salt (½ teaspoon if broth is salty), and chicken; stir and bring to a boil. Cover the pan, reduce heat to low, and cook for 25 minutes. Remove the pan from the heat. Remove the lid, mix in peas, cover, and wait for 5 minutes. Serve.

Nutrition Information
Amounts per Serving

Calories: 187
Calories from fat: 23.0%
Total fat: 4.9 g
Saturated fat: 0.9 g

Cholesterol: 49 mg
Carbohydrates: 12.5 g
Protein: 24.1 g
Sodium: 569 mg

∾ Bifsteks a la Mexicana/Steak Strips in Spicy Tomato Sauce

Yield: 4–6 servings

Serve this simple dish with white rice, refried beans, and warm light flour tortillas for a healthy northern Mexican dinner.

Ingredients

1½ pounds (¾ kg) eye of round steak
1 teaspoon olive oil
3 cloves garlic, finely chopped
1–3 *chiles jalapeños*, thinly sliced
1 medium white onion, thinly sliced
1 can each whole tomatoes, 28 oz (784 g) and 14.5 oz (406 g)
½ cup (125 ml) chopped cilantro, loosely packed

Preparation

Trim the steak of all visible fat and cut it into thin strips about 5 inches (12.5 cm) long. Heat a large nonstick sauté or frying pan over medium-high heat. Add the meat and brown 3 minutes. Remove the meat and set aside; pour off and reserve drippings.

Add the oil to the pan used to brown the meat, reduce the heat to medium, and add garlic and chiles. Stir-fry for 1 minute, then add onions and reserved drippings. Stir, reduce the heat to medium, cover, and cook for 3–5 minutes until the onions are soft.

Drain the tomatoes, reserving the juice. Chop the tomatoes and add them to the pan. Stir, increase heat to medium-high, and simmer for 5 minutes. Add the beef and 1 cup (250 ml) reserved tomato juice. Stir, bring to a boil, cover, and reduce heat. Simmer for 45–60 minutes until the beef is tender. Remove the lid, stir in the cilantro, and heat for 1 minute. Season with salt; serve with plenty of sauce.

Nutrition Information	
Amounts per Serving	
Calories: 271	Cholesterol: 79 mg
Calories from fat: 27.4%	Carbohydrates: 16.1 g
Total fat: 8.4 g	Protein: 33.7 g
Saturated fat: 2.5 g	Sodium: 691 mg

∾ Albóndigas Enchipotladas
Meatballs in Tomatillo-Chipotle Sauce

Yield: 6 servings

This is a common lunch item served in *cocinas económicas* throughout Mexico and a must for anyone who enjoys the smoky sting of the *chipotle*. Serve with corn tortillas, rice, and a vegetable side dish.

Meatball Ingredients

1 ½ pounds (¾ kg) extra-lean ground turkey or extra-lean ground beef
4 cloves garlic, minced
½ medium onion, finely chopped
1–3 *chiles serranos*, finely chopped
½ teaspoon dried rosemary
1 teaspoon dried oregano
⅓ cup (80 ml) chopped fresh cilantro, loosely packed
⅓ cup (80 ml) chopped fresh Italian parsley, loosely packed
¼ cup (60 ml) chopped fresh mint, loosely packed, or 1 ½ teaspoons dried mint
¼ cup (60 ml) bread crumbs

Salsa Ingredients

5 tomatillos, with husks and stems removed
3 large tomatoes
1 tablespoon corn oil
1 slice white onion, ¼-inch thick (0.5-cm)
1 clove garlic, finely chopped
3–6 canned *chiles chipotles* in *adobo*
½ teaspoon ground toasted cumin seed or powdered cumin
½ teaspoon salt

Preparation

Prepare meatballs. Preheat oven to 375°F (190°C). Combine turkey (or beef), garlic, onion, *chiles serranos*, and herbs in a large bowl. Add bread crumbs, mix well, and form the mixture into eighteen balls 1 ½ inches (3.75 cm) in diameter. Put the balls on a rimmed baking sheet coated with cooking spray and bake for 30 minutes; turn meatballs over after 15 minutes.

Prepare salsa. Put tomatillos and tomatoes in a large saucepan and cover with water. Bring to a boil, lower heat, and simmer for 10 minutes. Drain; reserve cooking water. Heat the oil in a small saucepan. Add the onion slice and blacken over medium heat. Put tomatillos, tomatoes, garlic, and *chiles chipotles* with some *adobo* sauce in a blender. Add 1 cup (250 ml) reserved cooking water and purée.

Add the contents of the blender to the pan and bring to a simmer. Add cumin and salt, and simmer vigorously for 15 minutes, stirring frequently. Reduce the heat if the sauce begins to spatter. Remove the meatballs from the oven and add to the pan. Simmer for 2–3 minutes; serve three meatballs per person, topped with plenty of sauce.

Nutrition Information: Turkey Meatballs
Amounts per Serving

Calories: 239
Calories from fat: 17.0%
Total fat: 4.7 g
Saturated fat: 0.9 g

Cholesterol: 55 mg
Carbohydrates: 20.6 g
Protein: 31.5 g
Sodium: 364 mg

Nutrition Information: Beef Meatballs
Amounts per Serving

Calories: 263
Calories from fat: 31.9%
Total fat: 8.4 g
Saturated fat: 2.5 g

Cholesterol: 60 mg
Carbohydrates: 22.9 g
Protein: 17.5 g
Sodium: 618 mg

༺ *Pavo en Relleno Blanco*
Turkey in a White Sauce

Yield: 6 servings

This is a favorite dish in Yucatán, where turkey farms are surprisingly common.

Ingredients

2 pounds (1 kg) turkey tenderloins, cut into ½-inch-thick (1.25-cm) steaks
1 lime, quartered
2 cloves garlic, crushed
Salsa de Jitomate (recipe follows)
Salsa Blanca (recipe follows)

Salsa de Jitomate Ingredients

2 teaspoons corn oil
1 medium white onion, chopped
2 *chiles serranos*, chopped
3 large ripe tomatoes, chopped
1 teaspoon chopped fresh Italian parsley
2 tablespoons raisins
1 tablespoon capers, drained
5 green olives, pitted and sliced
2 tablespoons slivered almonds
Salt and pepper, to taste

Salsa Blanca Ingredients

3 cups (750 ml) *Caldo de Pollo* (pages 160–161) or canned clear chicken broth
½ cup (125 ml) white flour
1 cup *Salsa de Jitomate*
Pinch of white pepper

Preparation

Preheat oven to 375°F (190°C). Rub the turkey steaks with lime and garlic. Place the turkey in a baking dish coated lightly with cooking spray and bake for 30 minutes, turning steaks over at 15 minutes.

Prepare *Salsa de Jitomate*. Heat the oil in a nonstick frying pan over medium-low heat. Add the onion and chiles, and sauté for 6–8 minutes until the onion is soft but not brown. Add tomatoes, parsley, raisins, capers, olives, and almonds. Stir, season with salt and pepper, and simmer for 10 minutes, stirring frequently.

Prepare *Salsa Blanca*. Put the broth in a saucepan, add flour, and bring to a boil, stirring constantly. When the sauce has thickened, add *Salsa de Jitomate* and white pepper; stir and reduce the heat to low.

Remove the turkey from the oven and serve 1 steak per person, topped with plenty of *Salsa Blanca*. Put the remaining (warm) *Salsa de Jitomate* in a bowl and serve on the side, to be added individually *al gusto*.

Nutrition Information
Amounts per Serving

Calories: 306	Cholesterol: 98 mg
Calories from fat: 25.2%	Carbohydrates: 19.2 g
Total fat: 8.5 g	Protein: 37.9 g
Saturated fat: 2.0 g	Sodium: 511 mg

❧ Budín Azteca
Aztec Pie or Mexican Lasagna

Yield: 4–6 servings

In Mexican cuisine, a *budín*, which means pudding, may refer to a sweet dessert or a hearty casserole such as this famous dish.

Ingredients
6 *chiles poblanos* or Anaheim peppers
3 large split chicken breasts
1 small white onion, thinly sliced
15 corn tortillas, 5 inches (12.5 cm) in diameter
Salsa Verde Cocida (page 51)
½ cup (60 ml) light sour cream thinned with 2 tablespoons skim milk
¾ cup (185 ml) shredded reduced-fat mozzarella cheese
½ cup (125 ml) shredded reduced-fat cheddar cheese

Preparation
Roast and peel the chiles as described on page 19; remove seeds and veins. Cut the chiles into strips and set aside. Poach and shred the chicken as described on page 19; set the meat aside.

Preheat oven to 375°F (190°C). Cover the bottom of a square 2-qt (2-l) baking dish with 5 tortillas; cut some tortillas in half to cover the dish's corners. Spread half of the chicken evenly over the tortillas, then top with half the chile strips. Cover the contents of the baking dish with one-third of the *Salsa Verde Cocida*, one-third of the thinned sour cream, and one-third of the cheese.

Starting with 5 more tortillas, repeat this layering process. Top the second layer with a third layer of tortillas and the last of the *Salsa Verde*, sour cream, and cheese. Lay thin onion slices over the cheese. Bake casserole for 25 minutes uncovered until the cheese has melted and the sauce is bubbling from the bottom. Remove from the oven and allow to cool for 15–20 minutes. Cut into squares and serve.

Nutrition Information
Amounts per Serving

Calories: 426	Cholesterol: 72 mg
Calories from fat: 17.0%	Carbohydrates: 53.9 g
Total fat: 8.3 g	Protein: 36.8 g
Saturated fat: 2.9 g	Sodium: 779 mg

∾ *Calabaza con Pollo*
Squash with Chicken

Yield: 4 servings

This Mexican soul food is a slightly modified version of a dish introduced to me by Austinite María Delgado—professional, mother, and cook.

Ingredients

2 teaspoons corn oil
3 cloves garlic, finely chopped
2 large boneless, skinless chicken breasts, cut into bite-size pieces
½ small white onion, thinly sliced
1 can whole tomatoes, 14 oz (392 g), or 2 large ripe tomatoes
3 medium-large zucchini squash (2 pounds or 1 kg), cut into ¼-inch-
    long (0.5-cm) slices and halved
1 can corn, 15 oz (420 g), drained
¼ teaspoon ground toasted cumin seed or powdered cumin
Salt and pepper, to taste

Preparation

Heat oil in a large nonstick frying pan or sauté pan over medium heat. Add garlic and sauté for 2–3 minutes until tender. Add chicken and onions and cook about 5 minutes until the chicken is done. Chop the tomatoes and add them to the pan. Bring to a simmer. Add squash, return to simmer, and cook for 5 minutes.

   Add the corn, cumin, and salt and pepper; stir. Cover and simmer for 5–10 minutes until the squash is tender and the liquid has cooked down a bit. Remove from the heat, and serve with or over white rice, accompanied by corn or light flour tortillas.

Nutrition Information
Amounts per Serving

Calories: 126	Cholesterol: 0 mg
Calories from fat: 19.9%	Carbohydrates: 24.4 g
Total fat: 3.2 g	Protein: 4.4 g
Saturated fat: 0.4 g	Sodium: 503 mg

∾ Chiles Rellenos de Arroz Integral
Chiles Stuffed with Brown Rice and Covered with Black Bean Sauce

Yield: 6 servings

This nutritious, meatless meal is packed with carbohydrates, protein, fiber, and vitamin C.

Ingredients

6 large *chiles poblanos*
1 ½ tablespoons olive oil
½ medium white onion, chopped
2 cloves garlic, finely chopped
2 cups (500 ml) long-grain brown rice
1 whole *chile serrano*
2 teaspoons salt, or to taste
1 ½ cups (375 ml) *Frijoles Negros de Olla* (pages 132–133) or 1 can
    black beans, 15 oz (420 g), with broth
Pinch ground toasted cumin or powdered cumin
½ cup (125 ml) crumbled *queso ranchero* or mild feta cheese as
    garnish
Chopped cilantro as a garnish

Preparation

Roast and peel the *chiles poblanos* as described on page 19. Slit each down one side, not quite all the way, and remove and discard the seeds and veins; set the chiles aside. Heat the oil in a large saucepan over medium heat. Add the onion and garlic and sauté for 2 minutes. Reduce the heat to medium-low, add rice, and stir-fry for 5 minutes. Add 4 cups (1 liter) water, *chile serrano*, and salt. Stir, bring to a boil, and cover. Reduce the heat to as low as possible and cook for 40 minutes.

Put the beans and broth in a blender and purée. Transfer them to a saucepan, season with cumin, and warm. Remove the rice from the heat. Remove the lid, fluff with fork, and cover. Wait 5 minutes, then stuff the chiles with rice. Serve one chile per person, covering each with plenty of bean sauce; top with cheese and cilantro.

Variations

Add peas, corn, or diced carrots to the rice sauté for a colorful twist.

❧ Enchiladas Suizas
Green Enchiladas with Cream

Yield: 6 servings

The name of this recipe literally means "Swiss Enchiladas," but like French dressing in the United States, there seems to be little connection between the dish and its namesake country.

Ingredients

4 large split chicken breasts
½ small white onion, thinly sliced
20 corn tortillas, 5 inches (12.5 cm) in diameter
Salsa Verde Cocida (page 51)
½ cup (125 ml) light sour cream thinned with 2 tablespoons skim milk as a garnish
½ cup (125 ml) crumbled *queso ranchero* or mild feta cheese as a garnish
Shredded iceberg lettuce as a garnish
Chopped fresh cilantro as a garnish
Cebollas Desflameadas (page 84) as a garnish

Preparation

Poach and shred the chicken as described on page 19; set the meat aside. Preheat oven to 375°F (190°C). Roll tortillas into enchiladas (see page 49), filling each with ¼ cup (60 ml) chicken. Bake for 8–10 minutes until the enchiladas are cooked but not crisped. Meanwhile, warm *Salsa Verde Cocida* in a saucepan. Remove the enchiladas and serve three per person. Cover individual servings with plenty of salsa and top with sour cream, cheese, lettuce, cilantro, and *cebollas*.

Nutrition Information
Amounts per Serving

Calories: 363	Cholesterol: 45 mg
Calories from fat: 16.5%	Carbohydrates: 52.0 g
Total fat: 6.8 g	Protein: 25.0 g
Saturated fat: 1.3 g	Sodium: 357 mg

∿ Enchiladas con Mole
Chicken Enchiladas with
Chile-Chocolate-Nut Sauce

Yield: 6 servings

Some of the best *Enchiladas con Mole* in Mexico are served at *Los Arcos de Belén* (The Arches of Bethlehem) restaurant in Cuatepec, Veracruz, ironically a city known more for its coffee than its cuisine. Not only is the *mole* there sweet and spicy, it's also copious, something quite uncommon for this labor-intensive delight.

Ingredients

4 split chicken breasts
20 corn tortillas
Mole Poblano (pages 98–99, steps 1-3)
¼ cup (60 ml) crumbled *queso ranchero* or mild feta cheese
Cebollas Desflameadas (page 84)
Cilantro, roughly chopped

Preparation

Poach the chicken as described on page 19. Set the meat aside. Preheat oven to 375°F (190°C). Roll tortillas into enchiladas (see page 49), filling each with ¼ cup (60 ml) chicken. Bake for 8–10 minutes until enchiladas are cooked but not crisped. Meanwhile, warm *Mole Poblano* in a saucepan. Remove enchiladas and serve three per person. Spoon plenty of warm *mole* over individual servings, then top with cheese, *cebollas*, and cilantro.

∿Tips

In my house, *Jalapeños en Escabeche* (pages 81–82) is the mandatory condiment for these enchiladas.

Nutrition Information
Amounts per Serving

Calories: 378	Cholesterol: 42 mg
Calories from fat: 21.2%	Carbohydrates: 51.4 g
Total fat: 9.0 g	Protein: 24.5 g
Saturated fat: 1.5 g	Sodium: 437 mg

ᗡ Enchiladas de Camarón y Jaiba Shrimp and Crab Enchiladas in Chipotle Cream Sauce

Yield: 6 servings

Fiery *chipotle picoso* is countered by rich *crema suave* in this distinctive coastal dish.

Ingredients
3 bay leaves
1 tablespoon salt
1 pound ($\frac{1}{2}$ kg) small shrimp, shelled
1 pound ($\frac{1}{2}$ kg) shredded cooked crab meat
Crema de Chipotle (recipe follows)
20 corn tortillas

Crema de Chipotle Ingredients
2 large tomatoes
8 medium tomatillos, with the husks and stems removed
2 *chiles anchos*, with the stems and seeds removed
1 clove garlic, chopped
2 slices white onion, $\frac{1}{4}$-inch thick (0.5-cm) each
2–4 canned *chiles chipotles* in *adobo*
$\frac{1}{4}$ teaspoon ground toasted cumin seed or powdered cumin
1 teaspoon salt
2 teaspoons corn oil
$\frac{1}{2}$ cup (125 ml) light sour cream thinned with 2 tablespoons skim milk

Preparation
Put 4 cups (1 liter) water, bay leaves, and salt in a large saucepan and bring to a boil. Add shrimp and boil for 2 minutes. Drain, chop finely, and mix with crab. Set aside.

Prepare *Crema de Chipotle*. Put the tomatoes, tomatillos, and *chiles anchos* in a large saucepan and cover with water. Simmer for 5 minutes and drain; reserve cooking water. Put the garlic and one onion slice in a blender. Add the tomatoes, tomatillos, *chiles anchos*, *chiles chipotles*, cumin, salt, and 1 cup (250 ml) reserved cooking water. Purée and strain into a large bowl. Heat the oil in a large saucepan over medium heat. Add the other onion slice; blacken, and discard. Add the sauce to the pan and simmer for 10 minutes, stirring occasionally. Reduce the heat to low and stir in sour cream. Keep warm over low heat.

Preheat oven to 375°F (190°C). Roll tortillas into enchiladas (see page 49), filling each with about 3 tablespoons shrimp and crab mixture. Bake enchiladas for 8–10 minutes until cooked but not crisped. Remove and serve three per person, covering each portion with plenty of sauce.

Nutrition Information
Amounts per Serving

Calories: 382	Cholesterol: 184 mg
Calories from fat: 11.3%	Carbohydrates: 47.1 g
Total fat: 4.8 g	Protein: 37.6 g
Saturated fat: 0.8 g	Sodium: 1050 mg

✎ Huachinango a la Veracruzana
Red Snapper in Tomato Sauce with Olives and Capers

Yield: 4–6 servings

This is Mexico's best-known seafood dish. One reason for its popularity is the versatility of the sauce. Cinnamon, clove, vinegar, dry wine, cilantro, citrus, pickled jalapeños, and even potatoes complement the basic tomato mixture well.

Ingredients
2 pounds (1 kg) red snapper fillets
Juice of 2 large limes
1 tablespoon olive oil
1 large clove garlic, peeled and thinly sliced
½ small white onion, chopped
1 can whole tomatoes, 28 oz (784 g)
10 pimento-stuffed green olives, halved
2 teaspoons capers
1 tablespoon chopped fresh oregano or parsley
1 bay leaf
Salt and pepper, to taste

Preparation
Put the fillets in a medium-sized baking dish and cover with lime juice. Set aside. Heat the oil in a large frying pan or sauté pan over medium heat. Add the onion and garlic and sauté for 3–5 minutes until the onion is soft but not brown. Drain tomatoes; reserve juice. Transfer tomatoes to a blender and blend coarsely, leaving some texture in the sauce. Add this to the pan, stir, and bring to a boil.

Preheat oven to 400°F (205°C). Add olives, capers, oregano or parsley, bay leaf, and reserved tomato juice to the pan; stir and bring to a boil. Reduce the heat, season with salt and pepper, and simmer for 8 minutes. Drain the fillets and return them to the baking dish. Pour the sauce over the fish, and bake for 10 minutes or until the fish flakes when tested with a fork. Serve with white rice.

Nutrition Information
Amounts per Serving

Calories: 263
Calories from fat: 22.5%
Total fat: 6.6 g
Saturated fat: 1.1 g

Cholesterol: 67 mg
Carbohydrates: 11.9 g
Protein: 39.2 g
Sodium: 538 mg

❧ Camarones Enchipotlados
Shrimp in *Chipotle* Sauce

Yield: 4–6 servings

Covering a vast expanse of the western Gulf coast, the state of Veracruz is home to many of Mexico's finest crops. Cacao, vanilla, coffee, tobacco, plantains, mangoes, papaya, tangerines, coconuts, and more all thrive there. But despite its agricultural prodigality, Veracruz is best known for wonderful seafood dishes like this one.

Ingredients
2 pounds (1 kg) large shrimp, peeled and butterflied
Pinch of salt
Juice of 2 large limes
1 tablespoon corn oil
1 small onion, thinly sliced
2 cloves garlic
2 peppercorns
4 medium ripe tomatoes, broiled and peeled, or 1 can whole tomatoes, 28 oz (784 g), drained
4–6 canned *chiles chipotles* in *adobo* sauce
½ teaspoon salt
3 tablespoons dry white wine
¼ teaspoon toasted dried oregano
¼ teaspoon toasted dried marjoram
Pinch of cumin

Preparation
Put the shrimp in a bowl. Sprinkle with a pinch of salt and cover with lime juice. Set aside to marinate for 20 minutes, then drain; reserve marinade. Heat the oil in a large nonstick frying pan or sauté pan over medium-low heat. Add the shrimp and onion, cook for 5 minutes, remove from the heat, and set aside on a plate lined with paper toweling.

Put the garlic, peppercorns, tomatoes, chiles, plus a bit of *adobo* sauce, and salt in a blender and blend coarsely. Add the contents of the blender to the pan and bring to a simmer. Add the wine, oregano, marjoram, and cumin; stir and simmer for 15 minutes. Add the shrimp and onions, stir, and simmer about 3 minutes until shrimp are curled and firm but tender. Serve with rice and beans.

Variations
This dish can be made with squid or octopus as well. Simply substitute 2 pounds (1 kg) squid or octopus, cut into bite-size pieces.

Nutrition Information
Amounts per Serving

Calories: 288
Calories from fat: 19.5%
Total fat: 6.2 g
Saturated fat: 1.0 g

Cholesterol: 276 mg
Carbohydrates: 17.8 g
Protein: 39.5 g
Sodium: 608 mg

❧ Cazón a la Campechana/Shark Stewed in Tomato and Onion

Yield: 4 servings

Located on the Gulf side of the Yucatán peninsula, the industrial city of Campeche does not offer much for the sight-seeking tourist. It does, however, serve up one mean shark stew—perfect for those unfamiliar with the exquisite flavor of shark meat.

Ingredients

1 pound (½ kg) shark steaks, trimmed and cut into large, 2–3-inch (5–7.5-cm) pieces
2 cups (500 ml) water
1 leafy sprig *epazote*, plus 2 teaspoons chopped *epazote*
1 tablespoon olive oil
1 medium white onion, thinly sliced
1–2 *chiles jalapeños*, thinly sliced
2 cloves garlic, minced
3 large tomatoes, broiled and peeled, or 1 can whole tomatoes, 28 oz (784 g), drained
½–1 teaspoon ground *chile piquín* or cayenne pepper
Salt, to taste

Preparation

Put the shark in a saucepan with the water and *epazote* sprig. Bring to a boil, reduce the heat, and simmer for 6–8 minutes until the shark is cooked. Heat the oil in a large nonstick sauté pan or frying pan over medium-low heat. Add the onions, *chiles jalapeños*, and chopped *epazote*; stir and heat for 6–8 minutes until onion is soft.

Put the garlic and tomatoes in a blender and blend coarsely, leaving some texture in the sauce. Add this to the pan, stir, and bring to a boil. Season the sauce with *chile piquín* and salt, reduce the heat, and simmer for 6–8 minutes. Add the shark, *epazote*, and cooking water, stir, and simmer for 3 minutes. Serve the shark in individual bowls, accompanied by rice and warm tortillas.

∾ Ostiones Guisados
Stewed Oysters

Yield: 4–6 servings

Oysters are a favorite shellfish, or *marisco*, of coastal Mexico. Eaten raw in cocktails or cooked in soups, stews, and sauces, they provide ample protein and contain little fat.

Ingredients

3 cups (750 ml) shucked fresh oysters, with liquid
1 tablespoon olive oil
1 ½ medium white onions, chopped
2 cloves garlic, finely chopped
1–3 *chiles jalapeños*, chopped
3 medium ripe tomatoes, broiled and peeled as described on pages 18–19, or 1 can whole tomatoes, 14.5 oz (406 g), drained
Pinch of cinnamon
6 pimento-stuffed green olives, chopped
2 medium russet potatoes, peeled, boiled, and diced
¼ cup (60 ml) dry white wine
½ cup (125 ml) chopped cilantro or Italian parsley, loosely packed
½ teaspoon salt, or to taste

Preparation

Drain the oysters, reserve liquid, and set aside. Heat the oil in a large sauté pan or frying pan over medium heat. Add the onion, garlic, and chiles, and sauté for 3–5 minutes until the onion is soft but not brown. Purée the tomatoes in a blender and add to the pan; stir; and bring to a simmer.

Add 1 ½ cups (375 ml) reserved oyster liquid, cinnamon, and olives to the pan. Stir and simmer for 1 minute. Add the potatoes, stir, and heat over medium heat 5 minutes, stirring frequently. Remove the lid, add and oysters, wine, and cilantro or parsley; stir; and simmer for 10 minutes until the oysters are cooked. Season with salt. Serve with beans, rice, and corn tortillas.

Nutrition Information
Amounts per Serving

Calories: 210
Calories from fat: 30.6%
Total fat: 7.0 g
Saturated fat: 1.6 g

Cholesterol: 74 mg
Carbohydrates: 22.8 g
Protein: 12.9 g
Sodium: 737 mg

～ Sopa de Mariscos/Seafood Soup

Yield: 6–8 servings

A trip to the Mexican coast should always include a bowl of hearty seafood soup seasoned with fresh lime juice and chile.

Ingredients

1 $\frac{1}{2}$ tablespoons olive oil
1 small white onion, finely chopped
4 cloves garlic
1 can whole tomatoes, 28 oz (784 g)
4 cups (500 ml) clam juice
3 cups (375 ml) water
2 bay leaves
2 teaspoons toasted dried oregano
$\frac{1}{4}$ teaspoon toasted dried thyme
1 tablespoon dry white wine
1 $\frac{1}{2}$ teaspoons salt, or to taste
1 pound ($\frac{1}{2}$ kg) medium shrimp, shelled
1 pound ($\frac{1}{2}$ kg) squid, cleaned and cut into 1-inch-thick (2.5-cm) rings
1 pound ($\frac{1}{2}$ kg) octopus, cleaned and cut into 1-inch-thick (2.5-cm) pieces
2–6 *chiles serranos*, finely chopped, as a garnish
4 limes, quartered, as a garnish

Preparation

Heat the oil in a stock pot over medium heat. Add the onion and sauté for 3–5 minutes until the onion is soft but not brown. Put the garlic and tomatoes plus their juice in a blender and purée. Add purée to the pot and simmer for 15 minutes. Add the clam juice, bay leaves, oregano, and thyme to pot. Stir, bring to a boil, cover with the lid slightly ajar, and simmer for 20 minutes.

Remove the lid, add wine and salt. Bring to a rolling boil and add the shrimp. Return to a boil and add the squid and octopus. Return to a boil once more, then remove the pot from the heat and allow soup to cool for 5–10 minutes. Set the chile and lime on the table, to be added inividually. Serve soup in large bowls, accompanied by fresh French bread or saltine crackers.

Variations

Substitute a pound of sea bass fillet or the like for a pound of shrimp and add it to the pot when you would have added the shrimp.

∾Tips

Do not cook the squid and octopus too long or they will become tough and rubbery.

Nutrition Information
Amounts per Serving

Calories: 327
Calories from fat: 20.3%
Total fat: 7.1 g
Saturated fat: 1.2 g

Cholesterol: 380 mg
Carbohydrates: 12.9 g
Protein: 49.9 g
Sodium: 637 mg

❧ Camarones en Adobo
Shrimp in Chile Ancho Sauce

Yield: 4–6 servings

Adobo is a versatile chile-vinegar sauce popular throughout the Spanish-speaking world. This Mexican version is also scrumptious with chicken or fish (recipes follow). Or, mix the *adobo* with ¼–½ cup (60–125 ml) orange juice and use as a rich enchilada sauce.

Ingredients

2 pounds (1 kg) large shrimp, peeled and deveined
1 teaspoon salt, or to taste
Juice of 2 large limes
6 large *chiles anchos*
½ cup (125 ml) white vinegar
1½ cups (375 ml) water
1 tablespoon olive oil
1 medium white onion, finely chopped
3 cloves garlic, chopped
1 teaspoon ground toasted cumin or powdered cumin
½ teaspoon ground oregano
¼ teaspoon ground thyme
¼ teaspoon cinnamon (optional)
2½ cups (625 ml) *Caldo de Pollo* (pages 160–161) or canned clear
   chicken broth
1 tablespoon brown sugar
3 tablespoons tomato paste
Pinch of salt

Preparation

Put the shrimp in a bowl, sprinkle with salt, and cover with lime juice. Set aside to marinate for 20 minutes; drain, reserving the marinade.

Slit each chile down one side. Remove the seeds and stems and discard. Spread the chiles out flat and toast in a nonstick frying pan over medium heat for 2–4 minutes per side until soft and aromatic.

Put the chiles in a saucepan with the vinegar and water. Bring to a boil, reduce the heat, and simmer gently for 6–8 minutes until the chiles are quite soft. Transfer the contents of the pan to a blender and purée; if the paste is too thick, add ¼–½ cup (60–125 ml) water and blend until smooth.

Heat the oil in a large nonstick sauté or frying pan over medium heat. Add the onion and garlic, and sauté for 3–5 minutes until the onions are soft. Stir in the cumin, oregano, thyme, and cinnamon, and heat for 30 seconds. Add the purée, stir, and heat for 2 minutes. Add the broth, bring to a boil, reduce the heat, and simmer for 5 minutes. Add the reserved marinade, brown sugar, tomato paste, and salt; stir; and simmer about 5 minutes until the sauce is fairly thick. Add the shrimp, mix well, cover, and simmer about for 10 minutes until the shrimp are pink and curled. Serve.

Variations

Pollo en Adobo: Preheat oven to 375°F (190°C). Put 6 large boneless, skin-less chicken breasts in a baking dish and cover with the *adobo*. Cover the dish with aluminum foil and bake about 1 hour until the chicken is cooked through.

Pescado en Adobo: Preheat oven to 400°F (205°C). Put 6 large whitefish filets in a baking dish and cover with *adobo*. Cover the dish with aluminum foil and bake for 45 minutes or until the fish flakes when tested with a fork.

Nutrition Information
Amounts per Serving

Calories: 289
Percent calories from fat: 19.8%
Total fat: 6.5 g
Saturated fat: 1.0 g

Cholesterol: 276 mg
Carbohydrates: 19.0 g
Protein: 39.9 g
Sodium: 1,274 mg

∿ *Caldillo*
Brothy Beef Stew

Yield: 4 servings

This filling stew from Chihuahua, a neighbor of Texas and one of Mexico's top cattle states, is traditionally made with steak or stew meat. Here, lean meat has been substituted to reduce the fat content to a reasonable level while maintaining plenty of flavor. Serve as a main course with light flour tortillas and a tossed green salad.

Ingredients

2 teaspoons olive oil
1½ pounds (¾ kg) extra-lean ground beef or extra-lean ground turkey
1 medium white onion, finely chopped
1 clove garlic, finely chopped
1 large ripe tomato, peeled, seeded, and chopped
1–2 *chiles jalapeños*, finely chopped
¼ heaped teaspoon crushed dried oregano
5½ cups (1¼ liters) beef broth
1 large potato, peeled and cubed
2 medium carrots, scraped and cubed
Salt and pepper, to taste

Preparation

Heat the oil in a large nonstick frying pan over medium heat. Add the meat, onion, garlic, tomato, and chiles and cook for 6–8 minutes, stirring occasionally, until the onion is soft but not brown. Add the oregano, stir, and transfer the mixture to a stock pot.

Heat the contents of the stock pot over medium heat. Add the broth, bring to boil, and cook for 6 minutes. Add the potatoes and carrots, and boil for 10–12 minutes uncovered until the vegetables are soft. Season with salt and pepper, let cool for 10 minutes, and serve, accompanied by warm tortillas.

Nutrition Information
Amounts per Serving

Calories: 340	Cholesterol: 21 mg
Calories from fat: 16.8%	Carbohydrates: 63.3 g
Total fat: 6.8 g	Protein: 12.7 g
Saturated fat: 2.2 g	Sodium: 1,409 mg

⌒ Pozole/Hominy Soup

Yield: 6 servings

Created in the west coast state of Jalisco, *Pozole* has become a national dish of Mexico. Each night, people throughout the country head to their local *pozolería* to relax and chat over crowded bowls of this exquisite hominy soup, which is traditionally made using a hog's head.

Broth Ingredients

2 ½ pounds (1 ¼ kg) ham hocks
3 split chicken breasts
1 medium white onion, quartered
5 cloves garlic, crushed
1 bay leaf
1 tablespoon salt
2 cans white hominy, 15 oz each (420 g)

Condiments

Ground oregano
Ground *chile piquín* or cayenne pepper
Finely chopped white onion
Lime wedges
Salt, to taste

Preparation

Put the ham hocks in a stock pot and cover with water. Simmer uncovered for 40 minutes. Meanwhile, poach and shred the chicken as described on page 19; set shredded meat aside.

Drain the ham hocks and rinse pot well. Return the hocks to the pot. Add 12 cups (3 liters) water, the quartered onion, 5 cloves garlic, bay leaf, and salt. Simmer uncovered for 1 hour.

Using a slotted spoon, remove and discard the hocks, onion, bay leaf, and garlic. Add the hominy and simmer for 15 minutes. Set the chicken, chopped onion, oregano, ground chile, lime, and salt on table in individual bowls. Serve the soup in large soup bowls; add toppings as desired.

Variations

Just about anything can serve as a *Pozole* topping. Raw shredded cabbage and sliced radishes are popular in Jalisco; cilantro adds a nice touch; and at one *posada* (a Mexican Christmas party) I was even given sardines to add to my soup.

Nutrition Information
Amounts per Serving

Calories: 332   Cholesterol: 45 mg
Calories from fat: 19.4%   Carbohydrates: 26 g
Total fat: 6.9 g   Protein: 39 g
Saturated fat: 1.8 g   Sodium: 507 mg

Chapter 6

Platos al Lado
Side Dishes

Due to the different styles of dining between Mexico and the United States, many secondary Mexican dishes don't fit into our familiar categories of a multicourse meal. For example, boiled beans, one of the most popular side dishes of traditional Mexican cuisine, are often served separately, as the *last* portion of the main course. On the other hand, rice dishes, known south of the border as *sopas secas*, or dry soups, are served at the beginning of the meal. And vegetables, which sadly are not a big part of the typical Mexican diet, may be served before, with, or as the main course.

In an effort to make meal planning easy, this chapter consolidates a group of recipes, excluding entrées, that are served between the (wet) soup and dessert of a Mexican meal. By serving one or two of these side dishes with a main dish or soup, and accompanying these with tortillas and the salsa or salsas of your choice, you can easily create nutritious Mexican meals within the framework of American dining. In addition, vegetarians can create healthy VegMex dinners by simply serving two or three of the following recipes with warm corn or flour tortillas and a favorite salsa or relish.

∾ *Frijoles Negros de Olla* and *Frijoles Pintos de Olla*/Pot-Boiled Black and Pinto Beans

Yield: About 5 cups (1250 ml)

Beans are the standard side dish of Mexican cuisine and are especially good low-fat food for vegetarians. Combined with corn tortillas, they provide the amino acids necessary for building protein. For a humble, nutritious meal, top a bowl of these pot beans with a pinch of cheese, chopped *chiles serranos*, cilantro, and onion. Serve with tortillas and salsa.

Ingredients

1 pound (½ kg) or 2 cups (500 ml) dried black or pinto beans
1 medium white onion, roughly chopped
8–10 cups (2–2½ liters) water
2 teaspoons salt, or to taste
1 leafy sprig *epazote* (for black beans only)

Preparation

Put the beans and onion in a heavy stock pot. Cover with water to about 3 inches (7.5 cm) above beans. Bring to a boil, cover with the lid slightly ajar, reduce the heat, and simmer for 1½–2 hours until the beans are just tender. Cooking time will vary, depending on the batch of beans.

Remove the lid and add salt; add *epazote* if cooking black beans. Stir and simmer about for 15 minutes until the beans are just tender and the cooking liquid has the consistency of a hearty broth. Add more salt if desired, stir, remove from the heat, and allow to cool for 10–15 minutes.

∾ Tips

Do not presoak beans as this robs them of nutrients and flavor. And do not salt them until tender, or their skins will toughen, and they will not soften.

If a thicker broth is desired, transfer ½–1 cup (125–250 ml) cooked beans to a blender, add 1 cup (250 ml) broth, and blend until smooth. Return the bean purée to the pot and mix. If a thinner broth is desired, simply boil the beans until just tender.

For *Frijoles de Olla* in one-third the time, cook the beans, onion, and 6 cups (1½ liters) water in a pressure cooker for 35–45 minutes. Release pressure, remove the lid and add salt; add *epazote* if cooking black beans. Stir and simmer about for 15 minutes until the beans are just tender and the cooking liquid has the consistency of a hearty broth. Add more salt if desired, stir, remove from the heat, and allow to cool for 10–15 minutes.

Nutrition Information: Pinto Beans
Amounts per Serving

Calories: 157
Calories from fat: 2.9%
Total fat: 0.5 g
Saturated fat: 0.1 g

Cholesterol: 0 mg
Carbohydrates: 29.4 g
Protein: 9.6 g
Sodium: 486 mg

Nutrition Information: Black Beans
Amounts per Serving

Calories: 158
Calories from fat: 3.7%
Total fat: 0.7 g
Saturated fat: 0.2 g

Cholesterol: 0 mg
Carbohydrates: 28.9 g
Protein: 9.9 g
Sodium: 484 mg

∾ *Frijoles Refritos*/Refried Beans

Yield: 6 servings

Served alongside meats, eggs, poultry, rice, seafood, and soup, refried beans are *the* side dish of Mexican cuisine. Whether you use black or pinto beans, they are also a great hold-me-over, eaten with a few tortillas and pickled peppers.

Ingredients

2 teaspoons olive oil
3 tablespoons finely chopped white onion
3 cups (750 ml) *Frijoles Pintos de Olla* (pages 132–133), with broth

Preparation

Heat the oil in a large nonstick frying pan over medium heat. Add the onion and sauté for 3–5 minutes until the onion is soft but not brown. Using a slotted spoon, transfer 2–3 spoonfuls of the beans to the pan. Increase the heat to medium-high and cook for 1 minute.

Add ½ cup (125 ml) bean broth to the pan. Using a wooden bean or potato masher (or the back of wooden spoon in a pinch), mash beans in the broth while cooking. When the beans have the consistency of a paste, add more beans and broth. Repeat this process until all the beans are mashed. Heat them to the desired consistency, then serve.

∾ Tips

To serve truly *a la Mexicana*, cook the beans to a thick paste, transfer them to a plate and stick 3–4 baked tortilla chips in them, upright in a row. Crumble a pinch of *queso ranchero* or feta cheese over the top, and serve.

There are many good canned nonfat refried beans on the market. Use them when you need a quick, no-hassle side dish.

Nutrition Information: Refried Pinto Beans
Amounts per Serving

Calories:171
Calories from fat: 10.4%
Total fat: 2.0 g
Saturated fat: 0.3 g

Cholesterol: 0 mg
Carbohydrates: 29.6 g
Protein: 9.6 g
Sodium: 505 mg

Nutrition Information: Refried Black Beans
Amounts per Serving

Calories: 172   Cholesterol: 0 mg
Calories from fat: 11.3%   Carbohydrates: 29.1 g
Total fat: 2.2 g   Protein: 9.9 g
Saturated fat: 0.4 g   Sodium: 503 mg

❧ *Frijoles a la Charra*/Pinto Beans with Onion, Chile, and Tomato

Yield: 4–6 servings

A scrumptious snack served with corn or light flour tortillas, *Frijoles a la Charra* are common in the regions just north and south of the border. This version comes from chef, musician, and full-blooded Texan, Jeffrey Grier.

Ingredients

1 tablespoon corn oil

½ medium white onion, chopped

1–3 *chiles serranos* or *jalapeños*, chopped

2 large ripe tomatoes, seeded and chopped, or 1 can tomatoes, 14 oz (392 g), drained and chopped

2 tablespoons roughly chopped cilantro

2½ cups (625 ml) *Frijoles Pintos de Olla* (pages 132–133), with broth

½ teaspoon ground toasted cumin seed or powdered cumin

Preparation

Heat the oil in a nonstick frying pan over medium heat. Add the onion and chile, and sauté about 2 minutes until onion is almost soft. Add tomatoes, stir, and heat for 2–3 minutes. Remove the pan from the heat and stir in the cilantro. Warm *Frijoles de Olla* in a large saucepan. Add cumin and the tomato mixture; stir; simmer for 2–3 minutes; and serve in individual bowls.

❧ Tips

Jeffrey Grier swears by adding a teaspoon of liquid smoke along with the cumin.

Nutrition Information
Amounts per Serving

Calories: 220	Cholesterol: 0 mg
Calories from fat: 13.5%	Carbohydrates: 38.3 g
Total fat: 3.5 g	Protein: 11.5 g
Saturated fat: 0.5 g	Sodium: 551 mg

∿ Arroz a la Mexicana
Mexican Rice

Yield: 4–6 servings

There are many ways to prepare this ubiquitous Mexican side dish. Use different vegetables: If fresh, add them with the carrots; if frozen, thaw and add them after fluffing the cooked rice. You might also add more garlic and/or onion, or use chicken broth instead of water.

Ingredients

2 teaspoons corn oil
1 rounded cup (250 ml) long-grain white rice
1 clove garlic
1 slice white onion, ⅛-inch thick (0.3-cm)
1 large ripe tomato, roughly chopped
1½ teaspoons salt
1⅔ cups (410 ml) water
2 carrots, peeled and chopped
⅔ cup (160 ml) peas, fresh or frozen and thawed

Preparation

Heat the oil in a large saucepan over medium heat. Add rice and stir until grains are coated with oil. Fry for 5 minutes until a few of the grains are brown.

Meanwhile, put the garlic, onion, tomato, salt, and 1 cup (250 ml) water in a blender, and purée. Add purée to the saucepan and bring to a boil. Add carrots and peas if using fresh. Simmer for 2–3 minutes until the carrots begin to soften. Add ⅔ cup (160 ml) water and bring to a boil. Cover the pan, reduce the heat as low as possible, and cook undisturbed for 25 minutes.

Remove the pan from the heat. Remove the lid and fluff the rice with a fork; stir in peas if using frozen. Cover, and allow rice to steam for 5 minutes, then serve.

Nutrition Information
Amounts per Serving

Calories: 117
Calories from fat: 12.5%
Total fat: 1.6 g
Saturated fat: 0.2 g

Cholesterol: 0 mg
Carbohydrates: 24.4 g
Protein: 1.3 g
Sodium: 647 mg

∾ *Arroz Blanco*
Rice Cooked in Chicken Broth

Yield: 6 servings

This dish would be served as a *sopa seca,* or dry soup, in Mexico. By any name, with its rich flavor and vivid appearance, it's always a crowd pleaser.

Ingredients

2 teaspoons olive oil
½ large white onion, finely chopped
2 cloves garlic, finely chopped
1½ cups (375 ml) long-grain white rice
3 cups (750 ml) *Caldo de Pollo* (pages 160–161) or canned clear chicken broth
1 teaspoon salt, or to taste
1 whole *chile serrano*
½ cup (125 ml) frozen peas, thawed
½ cup (125 ml) frozen corn, thawed

Preparation

Heat the oil in a large saucepan over medium-high heat. Add the onion and garlic, and sauté for 1–2 minutes until the onion is soft but not brown. Add the rice, stir well, and cook for 3–4 minutes until a few grains are brown. Add the chicken broth, salt, and chile; stir well. Bring to a boil, cover, and reduce the heat as low as possible. Cook for 25 minutes, then remove the pan from the heat. Remove the lid, add the peas and corn, mix lightly, and cover. Wait for 3 minutes, remove the lid, mix well, and serve.

∾ Tips

If you have fresh peas or corn, or both, add them with the broth and chile.

Nutrition Information
Amounts per Serving

Calories: 181	Cholesterol: 0 mg
Calories from fat: 11.9%	Carbohydrates: 35.9 g
Total fat: 2.4 g	Protein: 3.7 g
Saturated fat: 0.4 g	Sodium: 807 mg

❧ *Arroz con Chorizo*
Rice with Chile-Seasoned Meat

Yield: 6–8 servings

Served with salsa and corn or light flour tortillas, this recipe makes enough spicy tacos to feed a crowd.

Ingredients

Chorizo (recipe follows)
1 ½ cups (375 ml) long-grain white rice
3 cups (750 ml) water
2 teaspoons olive oil
½ medium white onion, finely chopped
3 medium tomatoes, chopped
Salt, to taste

Chorizo Ingredients

1 ¼ pounds (600 g) extra-lean ground turkey or extra-lean ground beef
8 medium *chiles guajillos* (6 inches or 15 cm long)
½ cup (125 ml) wine vinegar
6 cloves garlic
2 bay leaves
2 teaspoons dried oregano
½ teaspoon dried marjoram
½ teaspoon dried thyme
½ teaspoon paprika
6 cloves, crushed
8 peppercorns
1 teaspoon chile powder
1 teaspoon salt, or to taste

Preparation

Prepare *Chorizo*. Clean and soak the chiles (do not toast) as described on pages 19–20, reserving liquid. Put the vinegar, garlic, bay leaf, dried herbs, paprika, cloves, peppercorns, chile powder, and salt in a blender. Blend for 30 seconds until well ground. Add one-third of the chiles to the blender and blend until smooth; there should be no large bits of skin in the sauce. Add the remaining chiles and purée; add ¼–½ cup (60–125 ml) chile-soaking liquid if the sauce is too thick to blend. Add the contents of the blender to the meat in a large bowl and mix well. Cover and chill in the refrigerator several hours or overnight.

Combine the rice with the water in a large saucepan. Bring to a boil, cover, reduce the heat as low as possible, and cook for 25 minutes. Remove the pan from the heat. Remove the lid, fluff rice with a fork, and cover the pan.

Heat the oil in a large nonstick frying pan over medium-high heat. Add the onions and sauté for 2–3 minutes until almost soft. Add the tomatoes and cook for 2–3 minutes. Drain the meat and add it to the pan. Increase the heat to high and cook for 10–15 minutes until most of the liquid in the pan is gone. Reduce the heat to medium-low. Add the rice and mix well. Heat through, finish seasoning with salt, and serve.

Nutrition Information
Amounts per Serving

Calories: 315
Calories from fat: 11.4%
Total fat: 4.2 g
Saturated fat: 0.9 g

Cholesterol: 39 mg
Carbohydrates: 51.3 g
Protein: 22.2 g
Sodium: 271 mg

～ *Calabazas Guisadas*
Stewed Zucchini

Yield: 4–6 servings

Of the inestimable number of Mexican zucchini recipes, this is one of the simplest yet most satisfying.

Ingredients

2 teaspoons corn or olive oil
½ small white onion, finely chopped
1 clove garlic, finely chopped
1–3 *chiles serranos*, finely chopped
1 large ripe tomato, finely chopped, or 3 canned tomatoes, drained and chopped
2–3 medium zucchini (1 pound or ½ kg), diced
½ teaspoon salt, or to taste

Preparation

Heat the oil in a nonstick or cast-iron frying pan over medium heat. Add the onion, garlic, and chiles and sauté for 3–5 minutes until the onions are soft but not brown. Add the tomato and cook for 2 minutes, stirring frequently. Add the zucchini and ¼ cup (60 ml) water, cover pan, and reduce heat to medium-low. Cook for 6–8 minutes until the zucchini is tender. Remove the lid, season with salt, and cook about 5 more minutes until most of the liquid in the pan is gone, stirring frequently. Serve.

Variations

Add sliced mushrooms and a few fresh *epazote* or cilantro leaves to the sauté for a tasty twist.

～ Tips

Serve with chicken or seafood or over rice, accompanied by corn tortillas.

Nutrition Information
Amounts per Serving

Calories: 62
Calories from fat: 26.9%
Total fat: 2.1 g
Saturated fat: 0.3 g

Cholesterol: 0 mg
Carbohydrates: 10.2 g
Protein: 2.6 g
Sodium: 277 mg

∾ *Calabazas y Elotes a la Mexicana*
Squash and Corn with Tomato and Roasted Chile

Yield: 6 servings

This dish features a quartet of New World vegetables. Served with beans, salsa, and warm corn or flour tortillas on the side, it makes a quick, meatless meal.

Ingredients

3 *chiles poblanos*
1 tablespoon olive oil
½ medium onion, chopped
2 cloves garlic
1 large ripe tomato, chopped, or 1 can whole tomatoes, 14 oz (392 g), drained and chopped
4 cups (1,000 ml) diced zucchini squash
1 tablespoon water
1 package frozen corn (preferably shoepeg), 16 oz (448 g), thawed
½ teaspoon salt, or to taste
1 leafy sprig *epazote* or several sprigs cilantro
¼ cup (60 ml) shredded reduced-fat cheddar cheese

Preparation

Roast and peel the chiles as describedon page 19; remove the stems, seeds, and veins. Chop the chiles and set them aside. Heat the oil in a large nonstick or cast-iron frying pan over medium heat. Add the onion and garlic and sauté for 3–5 minutes until the onion is soft but not brown. Add the tomato and heat about 3 minutes until the mixture has thickened.

Add the zucchini and water, stir, and cover. Cook about 7 minutes until the squash is tender. Remove the lid, add chile and corn, and cook over medium heat for 1–2 minutes. Add the salt and *epazote*, stir, and heat until most of the liquid in the pan has evaporated. Stir in the cheese, cover, and remove from the heat. Wait for 3 minutes, then serve.

Nutrition Information
Amounts per Serving

Calories: 141   Cholesterol: 4 mg
Calories from fat: 22.4%   Carbohydrates: 24.7 g
Total fat: 3.9 g   Protein: 6 g
Saturated fat: 0.9 g   Sodium: 370 mg

∾ *Coliflor Poblana*/Cauliflower in Spiced Tomato Sauce

Yield: 6 servings

This aromatic dish is an excellent example of Pueblan cuisine, one of the most revered in Mexico. The clove, cinnamon, and olive reflect the Spanish influence on the state's famous cookery.

Ingredients

1 large head cauliflower
1 tablespoon corn oil
2–3 *chiles serranos*, finely chopped
1 medium white onion, finely chopped
1 tablespoon chopped fresh parsley
1 tablespoon chopped fresh cilantro
3 large ripe tomatoes, peeled and chopped, or 1 can whole tomatoes, 28 oz (784 g), drained and chopped
⅛ teaspoon ground clove
1 cinnamon stick 2-inches long (5-cm)
2 bay leaves
1 teaspoon capers
2 stuffed green olives, sliced
Salt, to taste

Preparation

Cut the cauliflower into ½-inch (1-cm) pieces and set aside. Heat the oil in a large nonstick or cast-iron frying pan over medium heat. Add the chile, onion, parsley, and cilantro, and sauté for 5 minutes, stirring occasionally. Add the tomatoes, clove, cinnamon stick, and bay leaf. Stir, reduce heat to medium-low, and heat for 1 minute. Add the cauliflower, cover pan, and heat about 10 minutes until the cauliflower is tender. Remove the lid, stir in capers and olives, add salt, and heat through. Serve.

∾ Tips

Serve as a main dish, accompanied by *Arroz Blanco* (page 138), *Frijoles Refritos* (pages 134–135), and warm corn tortillas.

Calories: 75
Calories from fat: 29.2%
Total fat: 2.7 g
Saturated fat: 0.3 g

Cholesterol: 0 mg
Carbohydrates: 12.1 g
Protein: 2.6 g
Sodium: 126 mg

❧ Espinacas con Papas y Garbanzos
Spinach with Potatoes and Chick Peas

Yield: 6 servings

Serve this colorful dish on the side for six persons or as a vegetarian entrée for four persons.

Ingredients

1 ½ pounds (¾ kg) potatoes, peeled
1 ½ pounds (¾ kg) fresh spinach
2–4 *chiles guajillos*
3 cloves garlic, chopped
1 medium white onion, chopped
1 teaspoon salt, or to taste
½ teaspoon sugar
¼ teaspoon ground toasted cumin or powdered cumin
1 can whole tomatoes, 28 oz (784 g)
1 tablespoon olive oil
1 can chick peas, 15 oz (420 g), drained

Preparation

Boil the potatoes for 30–35 minutes until they are tender. Drain, rinse well with cold water, and set aside. Remove and discard the spinach stems. Soak the leaves in cold water, rinse well, and set aside to drain.

Put the chiles in a frying pan and toast for 3–4 minutes over medium-high heat until they are dark on all sides. Remove them from the heat and cool for 5 minutes. Remove and discard the stems, then soak the chiles for 10 minutes in 1 ½ cups (375 ml) boiling water. Drain.

Put the chiles, garlic, onion, salt, sugar, cumin, and tomatoes with juice, in a blender and purée. Heat the oil in a large nonstick sauté pan or frying pan over medium heat. Add the contents of the blender and simmer for 5 minutes, stirring frequently. Chop the spinach leaves roughly, add to purée, and mix well. Cover the pan and heat for 5 minutes until the spinach is limp. Remove the lid and stir. Cube the potatoes into bite-size pieces and add them and the chick peas. Stir, reduce heat, and simmer for 10 minutes until the sauce is thick. Serve.

Nutrition Information
Amounts per Serving

Calories: 271
Calories from fat: 14.8%
Total fat: 4.7 g
Saturated fat: 0.6 g

Cholesterol: 0 mg
Carbohydrates: 48.4 g
Protein: 13.1 g
Sodium: 289 mg

∾ Chayotes al Vapor/Vegetable Pear Steamed in Its Own Juices

Yield: 6 servings

Juicy squash and fresh cilantro make this a perfect warm-weather dish.

Ingredients

1 tablespoon butter
2 pounds (1 kg) *chayote* squash, peeled and cubed
2–3 *chiles serranos*, finely chopped
½ cup (125 ml) roughly chopped cilantro
Salt, to taste (optional)

Preparation

Heat the butter in a large nonstick frying pan over medium heat. Add the *chayote* and chile and sauté for 3 minutes. Cover the pan, reduce the heat to medium-low, and cook for 10 minutes. Remove the lid, add the cilantro, and mix well. Heat for 3–5 minutes until the *chayote* is tender. Add the salt, and serve.

Variations

For a more colorful version, substitute 1 cup (250 ml) corn for 1 cup (250 ml) of *chayote*.

Nutrition Information
Amounts per Serving

Calories: 77	Cholesterol: 5 mg
Calories from fat: 25.7%	Carbohydrates: 13.6 g
Total fat: 2.5 g	Protein: 2.7 g
Saturated fat: 1.2 g	Sodium: 32 mg

∾ *Hongos a la Mexicana*
Mushrooms with *Epazote*

Yield: 4–6 servings

Like many Mexican dishes, these herbed mushrooms are unpretentious yet delectable.

Ingredients

1½ pounds (¾ kg) mushrooms
½ tablespoon olive oil
½ tablespoon butter
3 cloves garlic, finely chopped
4 scallions, chopped
1–2 *chiles serranos*, finely chopped
3 tablespoons roughly chopped *epazote*
Salt, to taste

Preparation

Halve the mushrooms lengthwise and set aside. Heat the oil and butter in a large nonstick frying pan or sauté pan over medium heat. Add the garlic, scallions, and chiles and sauté for 2 minutes. Add the mushrooms and *epazote*, stir, and cover. Cook for 7–9 minutes until mushrooms are tender. Remove the lid, add salt, heat uncovered for 1 minute, and serve.

∾ Tips

Substitute chopped cilantro if *epazote* is unavailable.

Nutrition Information
Amounts per Serving

Calories: 90	Cholesterol: 3 mg
Calories from fat: 28.3%	Carbohydrates: 14.1 g
Total fat: 3.3 g	Protein: 4.6 g
Saturated fat: 1.0 g	Sodium: 132 mg

❧ Papas en Salsa de Chile Pasilla
Potatoes in Chile Pasilla Sauce

Yield: 6 servings

This is one of those Mexican dishes that does not present itself well but tastes great. The seasoning of oregano and *chile pasilla* is a typical example of Mexican cooks combining Old and New World ingredients.

Ingredients
1 ½ pounds (¾ kg) potatoes, peeled
10 *chiles pasillas*
2 cloves garlic
½ large white onion, chopped, plus 1 slice white onion, 1/8-inch thick (0.3-cm)
1 ½ teaspoons dried oregano
¼ teaspoon dried marjoram
½ teaspoon ground cumin
Pinch of cinnamon
¼ teaspoon sugar
1 teaspoon salt, or to taste
1 ½ cups (375 ml) beef, chicken, or vegetable stock
1 tablespoon corn oil
1 ½ tablespoons wine vinegar

Preparation
Boil the potatoes for 30–35 minutes until tender throughout. Drain and rinse well under cold water. Let cool for 15 minutes, cube, and set aside.

Wipe whole chiles clean with a damp towel, then toast for 3–5 minutes in a nonstick or cast-iron frying pan until soft and aromatic. Transfer the chiles to a bowl and soak them in 1 ½ cup (375 ml) boiling water for 10 minutes. Remove the chiles, allow them to cool, and remove and discard stems.

Transfer the chiles to a blender. Add the garlic, chopped onion, herbs, spices, sugar, salt, and ½ cup (125 ml) stock and purée; if the purée is too thick, add more stock to thin.

Meanwhile, blacken the onion slice in oil in a large nonstick frying or sauté pan over medium heat. Add the purée to the pan, stir, and simmer for 5 minutes, stirring frequently. Add the remaining 1 cup (250 ml) stock, stir, and simmer for 5 minutes. Add potatoes, stir, and simmer for 10–15 minutes until sauce is thick. Add the vinegar, stir, and heat through. Serve.

Nutrition Information	
Amounts per Serving	
Calories: 160	Cholesterol: 0 mg
Calories from fat: 14.2%	Carbohydrates: 31.9 g
Total fat: 2.7 g	Protein: 4.9 g
Saturated fat: 0.4 g	Sodium: 573 mg

∾ *Ensalada de Col*
Mexican Cole Slaw

Yield: 6 servings

I discovered this warm-weather salad in Leon, Guanajato, a city more often cited for its quality leather goods.

Ingredients

½ small head green cabbage, shredded
2 large carrots, peeled and grated
½ small white onion, chopped
2 teaspoons olive oil
1 tablespoon Dijon mustard
2 tablespoons fresh lime juice
½ teaspoon sugar
Salt, to taste
Freshly ground pepper, to taste

Preparation

Put the cabbage in a large bowl. Cover with warm, well-salted water and soak for 15 minutes. Drain, rinse with cold water, and set aside for 15 minutes to drain. Transfer the cabbage to a large bowl. Add the carrots and onion and mix well. In a small bowl, mix the oil, mustard, lime juice, sugar, and salt and pepper. Whisk and pour over the vegetables. Toss, chill in the refrigerator for 20–30 minutes, and serve.

Nutrition Information
Amounts per Serving

Calories: 49
Calories from fat: 30.0%
Total fat: 1.8 g
Saturated fat: 0.2 g

Cholesterol: 0 mg
Carbohydrates: 8.1 g
Protein: 1.4 g
Sodium: 189 mg

ॐ *Ensalada de Ejotes*
Green Bean Salad

Yield: 6–8 servings

This tangy Mexican salad reminds me of one of my family's southern Italian recipes. Make it ahead of time and let it marinate while you work on the main course.

Ingredients

1 ½ pound (¾ kg) green beans, cut into 2-inch-long (5-cm) pieces
2 teaspoons olive oil
¼ cup (60 ml) white vinegar
1 teaspoon dried oregano
Salt, to taste
Pinch of sugar
½ large red onion, thinly sliced

Preparation

Toast the oregano in a dry skillet, as described on page 18. Steam the beans for 10–15 minutes until tender. Drain, rinse with cold water, drain again, and place in a large bowl. Pour the oil over the beans and mix well. Add the vinegar, oregano, salt, and sugar. Stir.

Boil 2 cups (500 ml) water in a saucepan. Add the onion to the water, stir, blanch for 5 seconds, and drain. Add the onion to the bowl, and mix with the beans. Marinate in refrigerator for 2–3 hours, then serve.

Nutrition Information
Amounts per Serving

Calories: 54	Cholesterol: 0 mg
Calories from fat: 24.1%	Carbohydrates: 9.7 g
Total fat: 1.7 g	Protein: 2.2 g
Saturated fat: 0.2 g	Sodium: 96 mg

∾ Ensalada de Chiles Rellenos
Chiles Stuffed with Tuna Salad

Yield: 6 servings

This is one of the many chile dishes of Mexico that feature tuna stuffing. Serve it as a substantial appetizer or as a light main course, along with soup and beans.

Ingredients
Marinade (recipe follows)
6 *chiles poblanos*
2 cans water-packed tuna, 6½ oz (182 g) each, drained
2 chopped scallions greens
½ stalk celery, chopped
2 tablespoons low-fat mayonnaise
Salt, to taste
1 small head romaine lettuce
2 roma tomatoes, thinly sliced
⅓ small red onion, thinly sliced
1 hard-boiled egg, chopped

Marinade Ingredients
⅓ cup (80 ml) water
⅓ cup (80 ml) wine vinegar
3 tablespoons fresh lime juice
1 tablespoon olive oil
2 cloves garlic, crushed
⅛ teaspoon toasted dried oregano
⅛ teaspoon toasted dried marjoram

Preparation
Prepare the marinade: Mix the water, vinegar, lime juice, oil, garlic, and herbs in a bowl. Whisk, cover, and let stand for 1–2 hours or overnight.

Roast and peel the chiles as described on page 19. Carefully slit each chile down one side, not quite all the way, and remove the seeds and veins, leaving the stems intact. Put chiles in a gallon-size (4-liter) zipper-lock bag, add the marinade, seal, and chill in the refrigerator for 2–3 hours. Drain the chiles; reserve the marinade.

Flake the tuna in a bowl. Add the scallion greens and celery, and mix. Add the mayonnaise, and mix well. Season with salt, cover, and chill in the refrigerator.

Stuff each chile with tuna salad and set on a platter lined with lettuce leaves. Top with tomatoes, onions, and egg. Whisk reserve marinade and drizzle over chiles. Serve.

Variations
Tailor the tuna salad to your taste. Mustard, lemon juice, shredded carrot, chopped artichoke hearts, chopped pickles, and olives all make nice additions.

∾ Tips
Use fresh key lime juice if available. Lower the fat count further by pouring only part of the marinade over the chiles.

Nutrition Information
Amounts per Serving

Calories: 126	Cholesterol: 52 mg
Calories from fat: 12.8%	Carbohydrates: 11.7 g
Total fat: 1.9 g	Protein: 16.7 g
Saturated fat: 0.4 g	Sodium: 253 mg

~ Ensalada Caesar/Caesar Salad

Yield: 6–8 servings

Invented nearly sixty years ago in Tijuana by Italian restaurateur, Alex Cardini, Ceasar Salad became popular at the San Diego Air Force base under its former name, Aviator's Salad. Over the years, this wonderful concoction has become a standard in restaurants across the United States. Try this super–low-fat version and it will become a favorite in your home as well.

Ingredients

1 large head romaine lettuce
2 small heads garlic
⅔ cup (160 ml) *Caldo de Pollo* (pages 160–161) or canned clear
  chicken broth
1½ teaspoons anchovy paste or 3 anchovies packed in oil, rinsed,
  and patted dry
2 teaspoons Dijon mustard
3 tablespoons lime juice
2 teaspoons Worcestershire sauce
2 tablespoons egg substitute
¼ cup (60 ml) grated parmesan cheese
Freshly ground black pepper, to taste
1 loaf crusty French bread, cut in 1-inch-thick (2.5-cm) slices

Preparation

Separate the lettuce leaves, rinse well, and set aside to drain. Separate the garlic into unpeeled cloves. Put the cloves in a medium saucepan, add stock, and bring to a boil. Reduce the heat, cover, and simmer about 15 minutes until the garlic is tender. Remove the pan from the heat. Remove the lid and allow the contents to cool.

Transfer the garlic to a plate, reserving the stock. Squeeze the pulp of each garlic clove into a blender; discard skin. Add anchovy, mustard, lime juice, Worchestshire sauce, and reserved stock to blender, and purée.

Pat the lettuce leaves dry, tear them into pieces, and put them in a large bowl. Toss the lettuce with egg substitute and garlic purée. Add grated cheese and pepper, and toss again. Serve, accompanied by slices of bread.

Chapter 7

Sopas/Soups

One of the best bargains on any Mexican menu, particularly for the weary traveler, is soup. For a handful of pesos, the tuckered tourist can recuperate with a delicious bowl of fresh ingredients simmered in a mild broth—the perfect restorative for a nerve-shattering bus ride through the mountains, a nasty bout of Montezuma's revenge, or both. And since soup is such an integral part of the Mexican diet, most restaurants offer a variety of four or five—and sometimes ten or more—selections to choose from.

Like other Mexican dishes, soups are typically served with fresh, colorful condiments. Lime wedges, salsa, chopped cilantro, *chile serrano*, and onion should all be set separately on the table for diners to add to their bowls *al gusto*. Also, although the recipes in this chapter are written as appetizers (serving six), the addition of a few warm tortillas will turn each into a satisfying low-fat meal for three to four people.

A word of warning about ordering soup in Mexico. The word *sopa*, or soup, can actually refer to one of two types of dishes: *sopas aguadas* (wet soups)—what we in the United States would simply call "soup"—and *sopas secas* (dry soups), which refer to rice and noodle dishes, so-named because they are cooked with soup stock. Tourists who order *sopa seca de arroz* in a Mexican restaurant expecting a bowl of light rice soup are often bewildered when their waiter brings them a plate of greasy seasoned rice. To avoid such confusion, the term *sopa* in this book refers only to *sopas aguadas*, the wet soups.

∾ Caldo de Pollo
Basic Chicken Stock

Yield: About 3 quarts (about 3 liters)

Often seasoned with a light tomato sauce or chile, this clear chicken broth is the basic stock of Mexican soup making and a wonderful pick-me-up combined with a little rice and shredded chicken (see Variations).

Ingredients

1 whole fryer chicken, about 3 to 4 pounds (1½ to 2 kg)
14 cups (3½ liters) cold water
1 carrot, quartered
1 large white onion, halved
3 large cloves garlic, crushed
8 peppercorns
1½ tablespoons salt

Preparation

Put the chicken in a stock pot and cover with water. Add the remaining ingredients, and bring to a boil. Lower the heat, cover the pot with the lid ajar and simmer gently for 4 hours.

Remove the pot from the heat and allow the contents to cool. Remove the chicken and save the meat for tacos, enchiladas, or other chicken dishes. Strain the stock into a large container and chill in the refrigerator for several hours or overnight.

Skim fat off the surface of the stock. Transfer the stock to a stock pot, bring to a boil, and strain. Use stock for soup or return it to a clean container and store in the refrigerator up to a week, or in the freezer indefinitely.

Variations

Caldo de Pollo Especial: For deluxe chicken soup Mexican-style, add some shredded poached chicken and plain boiled white rice to 6 cups (1½ liters) of hot *Caldo de Pollo* and serve, accompanied by warm corn tortillas, chopped onion, *chiles serranos*, and a wedge of lime.

∾ Tips

Some cooks include a few chicken feet with the fryer for extra flavor, while others add a little zucchini or *chayote* squash. Do not add parsley or celery, however, as this will de-Mexicanize your stock.

Vegetarians: Use vegetable stock with a little butter in it as a substitute for *Caldo de Pollo*.

Homemade bouillon cubes: Boil until the stock is reduced, allow it to cool, and pour it into a few ice cube trays. Freeze the cubes and transfer them to a freezer bag. Store in freezer.

Nutrition Information
Serving: Caldo de Pollo with 2 cups (500 ml) boiled white rice and meat of two split chicken breasts
Amounts per Serving

Calories: 161   Cholesterol: 17 mg
Calories from fat: 12.1%   Carbohydrates: 20 g
Total fat: 2.1 g   Protein: 13.6 g
Saturated fat: 0.6 g   Sodium: 797 mg

∿ Sopa de Tortilla/Tortilla Soup

Yield: 4–6 servings

Although tortilla soup is popular in American-Mexican restaurants, its sublime chicken-tomato broth is too-often smothered with an excess of cheese. This tasty, yet reasonable, recipe hails from Cuernavaca, a popular getaway spot for Mexico City residents.

Ingredients

15 white corn tortillas

Salt, to taste

2 *chiles pasillas* (optional)

6 cups (1½ liters) *Caldo de Pollo* (pages 160–161) or canned clear chicken broth

1 clove garlic

½ medium white onion, chopped

2 ripe medium tomatoes, chopped, or 1½ cups (375 ml) canned whole tomatoes, drained

1 teaspoon corn oil

1 large leafy sprig *epazote* (optional)

3 oz (85 g) reduced-fat mozzarella cheese as a garnish

¼ cup (60 ml) chopped cilantro as a garnish

Preparation

Preheat oven to 325°F (160°C). Pass each tortilla under running water, shake off excess water, and sprinkle each side with salt. Stack tortillas in two piles and cut into 1-inch-wide (2.5-cm) strips. Place the strips on two ungreased cookie sheets and bake for 20–25 minutes until they are crisp. Remove them from the oven and set aside.

Wipe the chiles clean with a damp towel. Lay them in a frying pan and toast over medium heat about 4 minutes per side until aromatic. Remove the chiles from the pan and allow them to cool. Slit each down one side and discard the seeds and stems. Crumble the chile bodies into a small bowl and set aside.

Bring the chicken broth to a simmer in a stock pot. Put the garlic, onion, and tomatoes in a blender and purée. Heat the oil in a frying pan over medium heat. Add the contents of the blender to the pan. Cook for 5 minutes, stirring occasionally, then add the mixture to the broth. Return the broth to a simmer and season with salt. Add *epazote*. Break the tortilla strips in half. Place 10–15 tortilla pieces in individual soup bowls, and pour hot broth over them, filling each bowl. Serve garnished with chile, cheese, and cilantro.

∾ Caldo Tlalpeño
Chicken and *Chile Chipotle* Soup

Yield: 6 servings

Seasoning broth with chile is classic Mexican cooking. This scintillating soup is wonderful as an appetizer or served with corn or flour tortillas as a light lunch.

Ingredients

2 large split chicken breasts
⅓ cup (80 ml) cold water
3 canned *chiles chipotles* in *adobo* sauce
8 cups (2 liters) *Caldo de Pollo* (pages 160–161) or canned clear
    chicken broth
½ cup (125 ml) chopped *chayote* squash
½ cup (125 ml) chopped zucchini or yellow squash
1 cup (250 ml) corn (preferably shoepeg), fresh or frozen and thawed
½ cup (125 ml) canned garbanzo beans, drained
½ cup (125 ml) chopped cilantro
Sliced avocado (optional)
Lime wedges as a garnish

Preparation

Poach chicken as described on page 19. Cut chicken into small pieces.

Put the cold water and chiles, with some *adobo* sauce, in a blender and purée. Transfer the purée to a bowl and set aside. Bring the broth to a boil in a stock pot. Add the vegetables and garbanzos. Season with salt, return to boil, and simmer about 10 minutes until the vegetables are tender.

Ladle the broth into individual bowls. Add ½ teaspoon chile purée, some chicken, cilantro, and a thin slice of avocado to each bowl. Serve, accompanied by lime.

Nutrition Information
Amounts per Serving

Calories: 130
Calories from fat: 12.6%
Total fat: 1.8 g
Saturated fat: 0.2 g

Cholesterol: 27 mg
Carbohydrates: 13.2 g
Protein: 14.8 g
Sodium: 1,339 mg

∾ *Sopa de Pasta*
Pasta in Chicken-Tomato Broth

Yield: 6 servings

The recipe for this basic Mexican favorite comes from Fortín de las Flores, a charming Veracruz city that was once a famous tourist spot for well-to-do Americans and Mexicans.

Ingredients

⅓ cup (80 ml) chopped white onion
1 large clove garlic
2 large ripe tomatoes, broiled and peeled, or 1 can whole tomatoes, 14.5 oz (406 g), drained
2 teaspoons corn oil
7 cups (1,750 ml) *Caldo de Pollo* (pages 160–161), or canned clear chicken broth
1¼ cups or 5 oz (300 ml or 140 g) elbows, ditali, tubetti, or other small pasta
Salt, to taste
Lime wedges as a garnish
1 white onion, finely chopped, as a garnish
1–3 *chiles serranos*, finely chopped, as a garnish

Preparation

Put the onion, garlic, and tomatoes in a blender, purée, and strain. Heat the oil in a stock pot or large saucepan over medium heat. Add the purée and cook for 6–8 minutes, stirring frequently, until well seasoned.

Add the chicken broth to the pot and bring to a boil. Simmer for 5 minutes, then bring to a rolling boil and add pasta. Cook for 6 minutes, stirring frequently. Season with salt and serve. Set the lime wedges, chopped onion, and chopped *serrano* on the table in separate bowls, to be added individually *al gusto*.

Nutrition Information
Amounts per Serving

Calories: 362
Calories from fat: 8.9%
Total fat: 3.5 g
Saturated fat: 0.4 g

Cholesterol: 0 mg
Carbohydrates: 68 g
Protein: 12.8 g
Sodium: 1,072 mg

∾ Sopa de Lima
Chicken and Lime Soup

Yield: 6 servings

This recipe from the Yucatán is perfect with an ice-cold beer, another specialty of the peninsula. Although its distribution is limited, Yucatán's brewery, *La Cervecería Yucateca*, makes the finest beers in Mexico: *Montejo*, crisp and full bodied; *Leon Negra*, dark and rich; and *Carta Clara*, light but tasty.

Ingredients

2 large split chicken breasts
½ medium white onion, chopped
10 corn tortillas
1 large ripe tomato, quartered, or 3 canned whole tomatoes, drained
2 teaspoons corn oil
7 cups (1,750 ml) *Caldo de Pollo* (pages 160–161) or canned clear
　　chicken broth
Salt, to taste
2 tablespoons fresh lime juice
3 limes, halved width-wise, as a garnish

Preparation

Poach chicken as described on page 19. Cut chicken into small pieces.

Preheat oven to 325°F (160°C). Pass each tortilla under running water, shake off excess water, and sprinkle each side with salt. Stack the tortillas in two piles and cut them into 1-inch-wide (2.5-cm) strips. Place the strips on two ungreased cookie sheets and bake for 20–25 minutes until crisp. Remove from the oven and set aside.

Put the chopped onion and tomato in a blender and purée. Heat the oil in a stock pot or large saucepan over medium heat. Add the purée and cook for 6–8 minutes, stirring frequently until well seasoned.

Add the broth to the pot and bring to a boil. Reduce the heat and simmer for 5 minutes; add the chicken, season with salt, and return to simmer. Stir in lime juice and serve. Float a lime half in each bowl and garnish with tortilla strips on the side.

∾ Tips

Use key limes if available.

Nutrition Information
Amounts per Serving

Calories: 178
Calories from fat: 19.0%
Total fat: 3.8 g
Saturated fat: 0.5 g

Cholesterol: 27 mg
Carbohydrates: 21.6 g
Protein: 14.6 g
Sodium: 1,207 mg

❧ Sopa de Elote/Corn Soup

Yield: 4–6 servings

There are dozens of variations of *Sopa de Elote* in Mexico, corn capital of the world. This basic version is based on a recipe from Los Arcos, a restaurant in the *zócalo*, or central plaza, of Cuernavaca. Serve as an appetizer for fish or chicken, or with a salad and crusty bread as a light, healthy meal.

Ingredients

1 tablespoon butter
4 cups (1,000 ml) fresh corn kernels (4–5 ears)
½ cup (125 ml) medium white onion, finely chopped
¼ cup (60 ml) water
2 cups (500 ml) *Caldo de Pollo* (pages 160–161), or canned clear chicken broth
1½ cup (375 ml) evaporated skim milk
Shredded reduced-fat mozzarella, Monterey Jack, or cheddar cheese as a garnish
Cilantro leaves as a garnish

Preparation

Melt the butter in a large nonstick sauté or frying pan over medium heat. Add the corn and onion, mix well, and cover. Cook for 10 minutes, stirring occasionally. Remove the lid, add water, stir, cover, and cook for 5 minutes. Remove the lid, add the broth, and bring to a boil. Reduce the heat, cover, and simmer for 15–20 minutes until the corn is tender. Remove the pan from the heat, uncover, and allow mixture to cool for 5 minutes.

Transfer the contents of the pan to a blender and purée. Pour the contents of the blender into a large saucepan and heat over low heat; slowly stir in the skim milk while the soup is heating. Continue heating the soup, without bringing to a boil, until warm throughout. Serve garnished with a sprinkling of cheese and one or two cilantro leaves.

Variations

Add a few *Rajas*, or strips of roasted green chile, (page 83) as a garnish for a robust twist.

Nutrition Information
Amounts per Serving

Calories: 172
Calories from fat: 13.5%
Total fat: 2.8 g
Saturated fat: 1.2 g

Cholesterol: 8 mg
Carbohydrates: 31.1 g
Protein: 9.3 g
Sodium: 408 mg

ꙿ Sopa de Nopales/Cactus Soup with Egg and Shrimp

Yield: 6 servings

I had all but given up on developing a taste for cactus when I stumbled upon this recipe in Pochutla, a coastal town in the state of Oaxaca. Not only is it the best preparation I've found for *nopal*, it's one of my favorite Mexican recipes outright. Serve as an appetizer with *Mole con Pollo* (pages 98–99) for an authentic southern Mexican dinner.

Ingredients

½ pound (250 g) cactus, cut into long, thin strips
3 large tomatoes, quartered
3 cloves garlic
½ large white onion, chopped
2 teaspoon corn oil
1 cup (250 ml) peas, fresh or frozen and thawed
1 sprig *epazote* (optional)
6 cups (1½ liters) water or clear chicken broth
Salt, to taste
2 eggs
1 pound (½ kg) small shrimp, cooked and shelled

Preparation

Boil the cactus 10 minutes in 4 cups (1 liter) salted water. Drain, rinse well, and set aside on a dish lined with paper toweling. Put the tomatoes, garlic, and onion in a blender, purée, and strain. Heat the oil in a stock pot or large saucepan over medium heat. Add the purée and cook for 8–10 minutes until well seasoned.

Add the cactus, peas, and *epazote* to the pot and heat for 1 minute. Add the water or chicken broth and season with salt. Bring the soup to a boil and simmer gently for 15 minutes. Beat the eggs, then slowly pour them into the simmering soup; the eggs will cook in the broth (as with Chinese egg-drop soup). Add the shrimp, heat through, and serve.

Nutrition Information
Amounts per Serving

Calories: 180	Cholesterol: 186 mg
Calories from fat: 26.5%	Carbohydrates: 11.1 g
Total fat: 5.2 g	Protein: 21.2 g
Saturated fat: 1.0 g	Sodium: 1,099 mg

⌣ *Crema de Calabaza*
Cream of Zucchini Soup

Yield: 6 servings

Mexicans love to make cream soups out of just about any vegetable. Carrots, asparagus, broccoli, or yellow squash can all be substituted for the zucchini used here. Served with a fresh loaf of French bread, each version makes a superb light meal.

Ingredients

4–5 medium zucchini (1 ½ pounds or ¾ kg), cubed
1 tablespoon butter
½ large white onion, finely chopped
2 cloves garlic, finely chopped
¼ cup (60 ml) chopped Italian parsley or cilantro
1 ½ cups (375 ml) *Caldo de Pollo* (pages 160–161), canned clear
     chicken broth, vegetable broth, or water
½ cup (125 ml) evaporated skim milk
1 teaspoon salt, or to taste

Preparation

Put the zucchini in a large saucepan, cover with water and bring to a boil. Lower the heat, simmer about 15 minutes or until the zucchini cubes are soft, then remove the pan from the heat. Allow the zucchini to cool in cooking water. Melt the butter in a small saucepan over medium heat. Add the onion and garlic, cover, and cook for 2 minutes until soft but not brown. Remove the lid, stir in the parsley, cover, and cook for 2 minutes.

Transfer the onion mixture to a blender. Add the zucchini, ½ cup (125 ml) zucchini cooking water, and salt to the blender and purée. Pour the contents of the blender into a large saucepan and heat over medium heat. Add the chicken broth or water, stir, and bring to a low simmer. Slowly stir in evaporated milk. Season with salt, heat through, and serve.

Nutrition Information
Amounts per Serving

Calories: 72	Cholesterol: 2 mg
Calories from fat: 27.0%	Carbohydrates: 9 g
Total fat: 2.3 g	Protein: 5 g
Saturated fat: 0.4 g	Sodium: 304 mg

❧ *Caldo de Hongos*
Spicy Mushroom Soup

Yield: 6 servings

Although much of Mexico is tropically hot, some areas, such as the mountainous Veracruz, can get quite chilly. A cold front rolling in from the north, called a *norte* by the locals, can turn a balmy morning into a blustery afternoon and a downright nasty evening. During one drizzly cold spell, the *muchacha*, or maid, of my friend's home helped us combat the inclement weather with this spicy, satisfying soup.

Ingredients

1 tablespoon corn oil
2 medium white onions, thinly sliced
4–8 whole *chiles de árbol*
2 cloves garlic, finely chopped
1 ¼ pounds (600 g) button mushrooms, thinly sliced
3 cups (750 ml) water
4 cups (1,000 ml) *Caldo de Pollo* (pages 160–161) or canned clear
   chicken broth
Salt, to taste
½ cup (125 ml) chopped cilantro, loosely packed
Chopped scallions as a garnish

Preparation

Heat the oil in a stock pot over medium heat. Add the onions, chiles, and garlic, and cook for 5 minutes, stirring frequently. Add the mushrooms, water, and 2 cups (500 ml) of the broth; stir; and bring to a boil. Reduce the heat and simmer for 5 minutes.

Add the remaining 2 cups (500 ml) broth and return the soup to a simmer. Season with salt. Add the cilantro and heat for 2 minutes. Serve garnished with scallions.

Nutrition Information
Amounts per Serving

Calories: 80	Cholesterol: 0 mg
Calories from fat: 30.0%	Carbohydrates: 11.9 g
Total fat: 3.0 g	Protein: 3.6 g
Saturated fat: 0.3 g	Sodium: 806 mg

∾ *Sopa de Frijol Negro*
Black Bean Soup

Yield: 6 servings

This hearty soup is common in southern Mexico, where black beans are most popular. Occasionally, I'll give it a *Yucateco* accent by mixing in a few tablespoons of *Salsa del Infierno* (page 80) in the final 10 minutes of cooking. Be sure to serve it with plenty of warm corn tortillas.

Ingredients

2 teaspoons corn oil
1 small white onion, chopped
2 cloves garlic, finely chopped
1–2 *chiles serranos*, chopped
2 medium ripe tomatoes, peeled and chopped
5 cups (1250 ml) *Frijoles Negros de Olla* (pages 132–133), with broth, or 3 cans black beans, 15 oz (420 g) each
1 leafy sprig *epazote* (optional)
Salt, to taste
Crumbled *queso ranchero* or grated parmesan cheese as a garnish
Chopped scallions as a garnish

Preparation

Heat the oil in a nonstick frying pan and sauté the onion, garlic, and chile over medium heat for 4–6 minutes until the onion is soft. Add the tomatoes and cook over medium heat for 5 minutes, stirring frequently. In two batches, purée the beans and broth in a blender. Pour the purée into a medium saucepan and simmer gently.

Put the tomato mixture in the blender with $\frac{1}{2}$ cup (125 ml) water. Purée, add to the beans, and mix well. Add the *epazote* to the soup and simmer for 10 minutes. Thin the soup with a little water if necessary. Season with salt and serve in individual bowls, garnished with a teaspoon of cheese and a few scallions.

Nutrition Information
Amounts per Serving

Calories: 115
Calories from fat: 16.0%
Total fat: 2.1 g
Saturated fat: 0.4 g

Cholesterol: 1 mg
Carbohydrates: 18.6 g
Protein: 6.4 g
Sodium: 460 mg

❧ *Sopa de Habas*/Fava Bean Soup

Yield: 6 servings

This thick bean soup is based on one I sampled at Los Vikingos restaurant in Cuernavaca, Morelos, during lunch with a few friends. It doesn't look like much—*mis amigos* were afraid to taste it—but the flavor is divine.

Ingredients

11 cups (2¾ liters) water
¾ pounds (300 g) or 2 cups (500 ml) dried fava beans
1 medium white onion, chopped
4 cloves garlic, chopped
½ cup (125 ml) chopped cilantro
2 teaspoons salt, or to taste
6 cilantro sprigs as a garnish

Preparation

Put the water in a stock pot and bring to a boil. Add all the ingredients except the salt, stir and simmer gently for 2–2½ hours, uncovered, until beans are soft and disintegrating. When the soup has a fairly thick consistency—almost like a purée—season it with salt, then remove it from the heat and serve garnished with cilantro sprigs. Serve with fresh French bread.

❧ Tips

Stir frequently during the last half hour of cooking to avoid burning the soup.

Nutrition Information
Amounts per Serving

Calories: 55	Cholesterol: 0 mg
Calories from fat: 7.6%	Carbohydrates: 9.5 g
Total fat: 0.5 g	Protein: 4.0 g
Saturated fat: 0.1 g	Sodium: 582 mg

∾ *Sopa de Espinacas y Coditos* Spinach and Elbow Macaroni Soup

Yield: 6 servings

This pasta soup is a recipe from one of the many outstanding restaurants of Zihuatanejo, a fishing-village-turned-tourist-spot located 200 kilometers west of Acapulco. There are many European influences in this coastal town, from French bakeries to Italian restaurants, and I'm still not sure from where this soup claims its origin. Nevertheless, I noticed plenty of natives eating it, so I figure it is Mexican in appeal.

Ingredients

2 teaspoons corn oil
½ large white onion, finely chopped
3 cloves garlic, finely chopped
2 ripe medium tomatoes, peeled and chopped, or 3–4 canned whole
   tomatoes, drained and chopped
6 cups (1½ liters) *Caldo de Pollo* (pages 160–161) or canned clear
   chicken broth
1½ cups (375 ml) elbow macaroni (4 oz or 112 g)
4 cups (1,000 ml) chopped spinach, loosely packed
Salt, to taste
Chopped scallion as a garnish

Preparation

Heat the oil in a nonstick frying pan over medium heat. Add the onion and garlic and sauté for 3–5 minutes until the onion is soft but not brown. Add the tomatoes and cook for 3 minutes, stirring frequently. Transfer the contents of the pan to a stock pot, add the broth, and simmer vigorously for 3 minutes.

Bring the broth to a rolling boil, add the pasta, and cook for 5 minutes, stirring occasionally. Add the spinach and cook for 1 minute. Season the soup with salt and serve garnished with scallions.

Nutrition Information
Amounts per Serving

Calories: 119　　　　Cholesterol: 0 mg
Calories from fat: 19.7%　　Carbohydrates: 19.2 g
Total fat: 2.7 g　　　　Protein: 5.2 g
Saturated fat: 0.3 g　　　Sodium: 992 mg

❧ Caldo de Gato/Vegetable Soup

Yield: 6 servings

The name of this throw-together Oaxacan soup literally means "cat's soup." It is excellent as a vegetarian appetizer—or, for a filling and healthy dinner that serves four, add beef or chicken (recipe follows) and serve it with a loaf of French bread and a tossed salad.

Ingredients

2 quarts (1 ¾ liters) *Caldo de Pollo* (pages 160–161) or canned vegetable, beef, or chicken stock
1 cup (250 ml) fresh green beans, cut into 2-inch-long (5-cm) pieces
2 carrots, peeled and sliced into rounds or ovals
1 cup (250 ml) cubed *chayote* or zucchini squash
1 cup (250 ml) cubed peeled potato
4 whole *chiles güeros* or *jalapeños*
1 cup (250 ml) canned garbanzo beans, drained
Salt, to taste
1 medium tomato, seeded and finely chopped
⅔ cup (160 ml) chopped fresh cilantro leaves, loosely packed

Preparation

Bring the stock to a boil in a stock pot. Add the green beans, return to a boil, and cook for 1 minute. Add the carrots, return to a boil, and cook 1 minute. Add the *chayote*, potato, and chiles; return to a boil; reduce the heat; and simmer for 10 minutes. Add the garbanzos, season with salt, stir in the tomato, and simmer for 5 minutes. Add the cilantro, heat for 2 minutes, and serve.

Variations

Caldo de Gato con Res: Use beef stock. Bring to a boil and add 1 pound (½ kg) trimmed lean beef, cut into 1-inch (2.5-cm) cubes. Reduce the heat, cover, and simmer for 1 hour before adding vegetables as above.

Caldo de Gato con Pollo: Use homemade or canned chicken stock. Bring to a boil and add 1 pound (½ kg) boneless, skinless chicken breast, cut into 1-inch (2.5-cm) cubes. Bring to a boil and add vegetables as above.

Nutrition Information
Amounts per Serving

Calories: 188	Cholesterol: 0 mg
Calories from fat: 11.9%	Carbohydrates: 34.2 g
Total fat: 2.7 g	Protein: 10.3 g
Saturated fat: 0.4 g	Sodium: 1,577 mg

Chapter 8

Botanas/Snacks

One of the most difficult times to avoid eating fat-filled foods is when having a few drinks. As the night moves along and spirits dissolve willpower, the greasy fare at the buffet table starts to beckon irresistibly. In horror, you watch yourself as you down a glistening cocktail weenie, knowing you'll be sorry in the morning.

The following selection of light hors d'oeuvres can help you battle the munchies at your next cocktail party. The dishes are what might be called *botanas* in Mexico. *Botanas* are served in many restaurants; patrons pay only for drinks (usually at slightly inflated prices), and a plethora of tasty tidbits is brought to the table. The *botanas* that follow are wonderful by themselves, accompanied by a few beers, margaritas, or other *copas* (mixed drinks), or served as exquisite appetizers.

❧ Ceviche
Fish in Tomato-Lime Salsa

Yield: 6 servings

Invented in Acapulco, *Ceviche* has become a standard dish in practically every coastal town of Mexico. Small pieces of fish are first cooked chemically with the citric acid found in lime juice, then rinsed and mixed with a salsa base (which, yes, does traditionally contain ketchup). Alternatively, if you're squeamish about eating lime-cooked fish, cut some yellowfin tuna into ½-inch (1-cm) pieces and boil it until firm, in lieu of marinating the diced or ground fillets.

Ingredients

1 pound (½ kg) fresh red snapper fillets (see Tips)
1½ cups (375 ml) fresh lime juice (10–12 limes) plus 1 lime
1 large tomato, seeded and finely chopped
½ large white onion, finely chopped
1–2 *chiles serranos*, finely chopped
½ cup (60 ml) loosely packed chopped cilantro
¼ cup (60 ml) tomato juice
½ cup (125 ml) ketchup
Saltine crackers and/or baked tortilla chips

Preparation

Dice the fillets or grind them in a food processor or meat grinder; transfer the fish to a nonmetallic bowl and cover them with lime juice. Cover the bowl and set it aside for 1–2 hours.

Drain the fish in a strainer and rinse with water. Transfer it to a large bowl, add the tomato, onion, chile, and cilantro; and mix. Mix the tomato juice and ketchup together, add to the bowl along with the juice of the remaining lime, and mix well. Chill in the freezer for 15 minutes. Serve, accompanied by crackers and/or chips.

Variations

Lay a few wedges of avocado on top of each serving for a traditional presentation.

❧ Tips

It is important to use fresh fish for *Ceviche*. Any flaky whitefish will work, including cod, orange ruffy, sole, haddock, and so on; use whichever is freshest.

Nutrition Information
Amounts per Serving

Calories: 138
Calories from fat: 7.8%
Total fat: 1.3 g
Saturated fat: 0.2 g

Cholesterol: 28 mg
Carbohydrates: 16.5 g
Protein: 17.4 g
Sodium: 356 mg

∾ Molletes
Bean and Cheese Melts

Yield: 6 servings

Molletes are Mexico's version of French-bread pizzas. Serve them as a light lunch or snack while watching a movie or The Game.

Ingredients

3 mini French loaves
3 cups (750 ml) *Frijoles Refritos* (pages 134–135) or 2 cans nonfat refried beans, 15 oz (455 g) each
3 ripe tomatoes, sliced
¼ pound (100 g) Monterey Jack cheese, thinly sliced
1 cup (250 ml) shredded reduced-fat mozzarella cheese
1 medium white onion, finely chopped
2 cups (500 ml) salsa of choice

Preparation

Preheat oven to 325°F (160°C). Cut the loaves in half and spread a generous layer of refried beans on each half; top with tomatoes. Cover them with Monterey Jack, then mozzarella cheese. Put the loaves on two cookie sheets and bake for 10 minutes. Remove; top each half with onions and salsa, and serve.

∾ Tips

Change the flavor of the *Molletes* by simply choosing a different salsa. The standard is *Salsa Mexicana* (page 70); *Salsa Ranchera* (page 52) and *Salsa Verde* (page 71) are also common favorites.

Nutrition Information
Amounts per Serving

Calories: 406	Cholesterol: 32 mg
Calories from fat: 20.6%	Carbohydrates: 52.6 g
Total fat: 8.9 g	Protein: 24.7 g
Saturated fat: 5.2 g	Sodium: 1,106 mg

⚖ *Quesadillas Estilo Mexico*
Mexican Grilled Cheese

Yield: 6 servings

Great with beer, margaritas, or *cuba libres* (rum and coke with a squeeze of lime), traditional Mexican *quesadillas* are fantastic finger food. Serve with your favorite salsa to spoon over the top or stuff inside.

Ingredients

½ pound (250 g) *queso oaxaca* or part-skim mozzarella, thinly sliced
½ pound (250 g) mushrooms, thinly sliced
Epazote leaves (optional)

Preparation

Make homemade tortillas (page 91) up to the stage of removing the tortilla from the press. Turn over the plastic/tortilla/plastic "sandwich," peel off the top piece of plastic, and lay the tortilla/plastic on the counter, tortilla side up.

Fill a small bowl with water and set aside. Place a couple slices of cheese, a couple mushroom slices, and an *epazote* leaf on one half of the tortilla. Starting at the side opposite this, peel the tortilla from the plastic and fold over the filling like an omelet. Dip your fingers in water and pinch together the tortilla's edges. Peel the *quesadilla* away from the plastic; set aside, covered by a dry dishtowel. Repeat this process until all the tortillas have been used.

Heat a nonstick or cast-iron frying pan over medium heat about 5 minutes until it's reached a constant temperature. Lay two or three quesadillas in the pan and cook for 2½ minutes until the facedown side is speckled with light-brown spots. Turn them over and cook for an additional 2½ minutes; press with a spatula after about 1 minute. Remove and keep warm, wrapped in a dry dishtowel, until all quesadillas are cooked—or serve immediately if the crowd can't wait.

Variations

Substitute any of the following fillings for the mushroom, or make your own combinations: onion, tomato, mashed potato, spinach, *chile chipotle* in *adobo*, and so on.

To make quick Mexican *quesadillas*, simply soften commercial white corn tortillas (page 20); fill with cheese, mushrooms, and *epazote*; fold and grill over medium heat in a nonstick frying pan coated with nonfat cooking spray.

∾ Tips

Cacique, a Californian company, distributes a serviceable *queso oaxaca*, which is lower in fat than most other cheeses.

Nutrition Information
Amounts per Serving

Calories: 395   Cholesterol: 20 mg
Calories from fat: 21.3%   Carbohydrates: 60.9 g
Total fat: 9.5 g   Protein: 18.3 g
Saturated fat: 4.5 g   Sodium: 205 mg

∾ *Vuelve a la Vida/*"Return to Life" Mixed Shellfish Cocktail

Yield: 6 servings

This mixture of seafood delicacies is common along the extensive Mexican coast. Like Japanese sushi, it seems to have a naturally intoxicating effect, although it is even better with a couple of frosty beers.

Ingredients

1 pound (½ kg) small squid or octopus, cleaned
1½ pound (¾ kg) medium shrimp
2 dozen large oysters, shucked and drained
4 cups (1000 ml) tomato juice
2 cups (500 ml) ketchup
Juice of 5–6 limes, plus 3 limes, quartered
Salsa del Infierno (page 80) or bottled *habanero* hot sauce
Salt and pepper, to taste

Preparation

Fill a large pot with water and bring it to a boil. Add half the squid or octopus, cook for 1 minute, remove, and rinse well with cold water. Bring the water back to a boil and repeat this process for the rest of the squid or octopus. Bring the water back to a boil again, add the shrimp, boil for 5 minutes or until the shrimp are pink and curled. Remove, and rinse well with cold water. Cut the squid or octopus into 1-inch (2.5-cm) pieces. Shell the shrimp, mix all the seafood in a bowl, and chill in the refrigerator.

Mix together the tomato juice, ketchup, lime juice, and a few dashes of hot sauce. Season with salt and pepper. Fill large soda fountain or cocktail glasses three-quarters full with cold shellfish. Pour the tomato mixture into each glass until almost full, then add another couple of dashes of hot sauce and serve, accompanied by lime wedges as a condiment. Use long spoons for eating.

Variations

Substitute half the oysters with a dozen fresh clams.

You can make a cocktail of any combination of the shellfish listed, or just one or two—for example, *Coctel de Camaron* (Shrimp Cocktail). Simply use a total of 3–3½ pounds (1½–1¾ kg) of seafood.

∾ Tips

Mexicans often serve this seafood cocktail accompanied by a small fresh salad made of 3 cups (750 ml) shredded green cabbage, 3–4 thinly sliced radishes, 1 cup (250 ml) loosely packed chopped cilantro, and ½ cup (125 ml) chopped white onion. Other tasty accouterments include *Salsa Mexicana* (page 70) and chopped avocado.

```
┌─────────────────────────────────────────────┐
│                                             │
│          Nutrition  Information             │
│           Amounts per Serving               │
│                                             │
│     Calories: 354          Cholesterol: 281 mg    │
│     Calories from fat: 9.0 %   Carbohydrates: 47.6 g │
│     Total fat: 3.8 g        Protein: 39.6 g       │
│     Saturated fat: 0.7 g    Sodium: 1,837 mg      │
│                                             │
└─────────────────────────────────────────────┘
```

∾ *Pico de Gallo a la Jalisciense*
Jícama Fruit Salad

Yield: 6 servings

Combining fresh fruit and chile is popular in Mexico. Serve this unique salad as an appetizer or a snack at your next cocktail party.

Ingredients

3 medium oranges
1 large (1½ pound or ¾ kg) jícama, peeled and cubed
2 large cucumbers, peeled, seeded, and cubed
⅓ pineapple, peeled and cut into bite-size pieces
Juice of 6 key limes or 3 regular limes
Salt, to taste
Ground *chile piquín* (optional)

Preparation

Peel the oranges and separate them into individual wedges. Carefully remove and discard the membrane encasing the pulp of each wedge, as well as any seeds. Cut each wedge into two or three bite-size pieces. Put the orange pieces, jícama, cucumber, and pineapple in a large nonmetallic bowl. Add the lime juice and toss. Chill in the refrigerator for 30 minutes. Remove, sprinkle with salt and chile, and toss again. Serve, with toothpicks, as finger food.

Variations

Toss the salad with ½ cup (125 ml) roughly chopped cilantro immediately before serving.

Nutrition Information
Amounts per Serving

Calories: 107
Calories from fat: 4.8%
Total fat: 0.7 g
Saturated fat: 0.1 g

Cholesterol: 0 mg
Carbohydrates: 27.5 g
Protein: 2.2 g
Sodium: 5 mg

❧ Arroz con Plátano y Salsa
Rice with Banana and Hot Sauce

Yield: 6 servings

I was actually served this dish at a *cocina económica* in Mexico City. I thought the waiter was playing a joke on me until I looked around and saw an old man digging in. Following his lead, I poured some salsa over the whole plate and found the contrasting flavors of the bizarre appetizer rather pleasing.

Ingredients

1 ½ rounded cups (375 ml) long-grain white rice
3 cups (750 ml) water
6 bananas, cut lengthwise in half
6 slices cucumber
6 slices pickled beet
2 limes, cut into wedges
Salsa Casera (page 73) or other tomato salsa

Preparation

Put the rice and water in a saucepan and bring to a boil. Cover, reduce heat as low as possible, and cook for 25 minutes. Remove from heat, uncover, and fluff the rice with a fork. Cover and leave undisturbed for 5 minutes. Uncover and let cool for 3 minutes; then prepare six plates of rice. Place two banana halves on each bed of rice. Garnish with a cucumber slice, a beet slice, and a lime wedge. Serve, accompanied by salsa.

Nutrition Information
Amounts per Serving

Calories: 466	Cholesterol: 0 mg
Calories from fat: 2.6%	Carbohydrates: 115.3 g
Total fat: 1.5 g	Protein: 7.4 g
Saturated fat: 0.1 g	Sodium: 894 mg

✒ Elotes
Mexican Corn on the Cob

Yield: 6 servings

Corn on the cob is one of the most popular street-cart items in Mexico. Street corners and town squares throughout the country are filled with vendors toting huge pots of *Elotes* to tempt hungry passersby.

Ingredients

1–2 tablespoons ground *chile piquín*, *habanero*, or other hot pepper
2 tablespoons salt
6 ears of corn, shucked
3–4 limes, quartered
1 cup (250 ml) low-fat mayonnaise (optional)
½ cup (125 ml) crumbled *queso ranchero* or mild feta cheese (optional)

Preparation

Put the chile and salt in separate bowls and set aside. Boil the corn in plenty of water until tender, about 10 minutes. Drain and allow to cool for 3–5 minutes. Roll a lime wedge in the salt. Rub one entire ear of corn with the wedge, seasoning the corn with as much salt as desired. Repeat this process with the chile using a new lime wedge. Dress the corn with mayonnaise using a rubber spatula, then sprinkle with cheese and serve. Repeat this process for the rest of the corn.

✒ Tips

The corn used for *Elotes* in Mexico is chewier and contains less sugar than most corn in the United States. Therefore, use corn that is not very sweet, such as shoepeg corn, for this recipe.

Nutrition Information
Serving: 1 ear
Amounts per Serving

Calories: 218
Calories from fat: 19.1%
Total fat: 5.2 g
Saturated fat: 0.8 g

Cholesterol: 3 mg
Carbohydrates: 43.7 g
Protein: 6.1 g
Sodium: 408 mg

Chapter 9

Desayunos/Breakfasts

Desayuno is the Spanish word for breakfast but this is misleading in Mexico, where there are two official mealtimes before noon. *Desayuno* is a light morning opener consisting of a roll or pastry, or perhaps a *tamal*, accompanied by fresh orange juice or *Café con Leche*. *Almuerzo*, literally "lunch," is a hearty meal served around 11:00 A.M. featuring a broader selection of dishes, including eggs, meats, beans, salsas, and tortillas. It is during this meal, which we in the United States would probably call brunch, that the recipes of this chapter would be served. Thus, although the following dishes are a wonderful way to start off the day (particularly on late weekend mornings), they are actually eaten in Mexico between our breakfast and lunch times. Of course, there's no rule against eating them anytime of the day.

∽ Huevos a la Mexicana
Scrambled Eggs with Onion, Chile, and Tomato

Yield: 4 servings

Serve this Mexican standard with beans and *Salsa Verde* (page 71) or *Salsa Mexicana* (page 70) for that extra kick. Serious chile freaks can add some *Jalapeños en Escabeche* (pages 81–82) as a relish.

Ingredients
4 medium eggs
1 cup (250 ml) egg substitute
2 teaspoons corn oil
½ large white onion, chopped
2–4 *chiles jalapeños* or *serranos*, finely chopped
2 medium roma tomatoes, seeded and chopped
8 corn tortillas

Preparation
Mix the eggs and egg substitute in a bowl, scramble, and set aside. Heat the oil in a large nonstick frying pan or sauté pan over medium heat. Add the onion and chile and sauté for 3–5 minutes until the onion is soft but not brown. Add the tomatoes and heat for 1–2 minutes, stirring frequently. Increase the heat to medium-high and add the egg mixture to pan. Heat, stirring occasionally, until the eggs are done. Warm the tortillas as described on page 20 and serve with the eggs.

Nutrition Information
Amounts per Serving

Calories: 292
Calories from fat: 26.2%
Total fat: 8.7 g
Saturated fat: 2.1 g

Cholesterol: 212 mg
Carbohydrates: 37.6 g
Protein: 17.7 g
Sodium: 322 mg

∾ Huevos Rancheros/Eggs on Tortillas in Tomato and Chile Sauce

Yield: 4 servings

I felt compelled to include an authentic rendition of Mexico's famous ranch-style eggs, contains a whopping 14 grams of fat. For a version lower in fat, use scrambled egg substitute or a combination of egg and egg substitute in lieu of the fried eggs. Serve with refried beans.

Ingredients
Salsa Ranchera (page 52)
8 corn tortillas, 5 inches (12.5 cm) in diameter
8 medium eggs
Salt, to taste

Preparation
Preheat oven to 375°F (190°C). Warm *Salsa Ranchera* in a saucepan. Place the tortillas on a cookie sheet and bake for 3–4 minutes or until warm. Remove and lay two tortillas on a plate; wrap others in a dry dishtowel.

Coat a nonstick frying pan with plenty of cooking spray and heat over medium heat. Fry two eggs sunny-side up and sprinkle with salt. Remove the eggs from the pan and lay atop the tortillas on the plate (one egg per tortilla). Cover the eggs and tortillas with plenty of sauce, and serve. Repeat this process for the remaining three servings.

Nutrition Information
Traditional style with fried eggs
Amounts per Serving

Calories: 412
Calories from fat: 29.5%
Total fat: 14.1 g
Saturated fat: 3.6 g

Cholesterol: 425 mg
Carbohydrates: 54.5 g
Protein: 21.4 g
Sodium: 776 mg

Nutrition Information
With 4 eggs and 1 cup (250 ml) egg substitute, scrambled
Amounts per Serving

Calories: 367
Calories from fat: 21.2%
Total fat: 9.1 g
Saturated fat: 2.0 g

Cholesterol: 212 mg
Carbohydrates: 54.9 g
Protein: 21.1 g
Sodium: 814 mg

ꙮ *Enfrijoladas*/Corn Tortillas Dipped in Bean Sauce

Yield: 3–4 servings

Filling, inexpensive, and absolutely delicious, these bean and tortilla treats are one of the best Mexican breakfasts. They are particularly popular in Oaxaca City, where each restaurant serves its own special version accompanied by freshly squeezed orange juice and coffee.

Ingredients

3 teaspoons corn oil
3 cloves garlic, finely chopped
1 medium white onion, finely chopped
3 cups (750 ml) *Frijoles Negros de Olla* (pages 132–133), with broth, or 2 cans black beans, 15 oz (420 g) each, with some broth
$\frac{1}{4}$ teaspoon salt
Pinch of ground anise
12 white corn tortillas, 5 inches (12.5 cm) in diameter
$\frac{1}{4}$ cup (60 ml) crumbled *queso ranchero* or grated parmesan cheese as a garnish
$\frac{1}{2}$ cup (125 ml) chopped cilantro as a garnish
2–4 *chiles serranos*, finely chopped (optional) as a garnish

Preparation

Heat 2 teaspoons oil in a large nonstick frying pan over medium heat. Add the garlic and half of the onion and sauté for 3–5 minutes or until the garlic begins to brown. Remove from the heat and transfer the garlic and onion to a blender. Add the beans and salt, and purée.

Put 1 teaspoon oil in the frying pan used to sauté the onion and garlic, and heat over medium-low heat. Add the bean purée to pan. Stir in the anise and cook for 5–7 minutes, stirring occasionally, until the sauce is thick and flavors have blended.

Reduce the heat to low. Using a pair of tongs, immerse a corn tortilla in the bean sauce. When the tortilla is soft (after about 5 seconds), fold it in half using the tongs, then into quarters. Remove it and place it on a plate. Repeat this process for each tortilla, serving three per plate. Top each serving with cheese, cilantro, peppers, and the remaining onions.

Variations

Enfrijoladas con Chorizo: Add some browned *chorizo* (pages 139–140) as an additional topping.

∾ Tips

To avoid making a mess, bring a plate to the pan when removing dipped tortillas.

Nutrition Information
Amounts per Serving

Calories: 473
Calories from fat: 12.9%
Total fat: 7.0 g
Saturated fat: 1.4 g

Cholesterol: 2 mg
Carbohydrates: 84.8 g
Protein: 21.2 g
Sodium: 1,029 mg

∾ Chilaquiles Rojos
Tortilla Strips in Tomato Sauce

Yield: 4 servings

Seasoned with chile and *epazote*, *Chilaquiles* (which allegedly means "broken up sombrero") are Mexican soul food at its finest.

Ingredients

20 corn tortillas, 5 inches (12.5 cm) in diameter
5 teaspoons corn oil
2 cloves garlic
3 ripe large (1½ pounds or ¾ kg) tomatoes, broiled
1–3 *chiles serranos*, roasted
½ teaspoon salt
½ cup (125 ml) *epazote*, roughly chopped
Grated parmesan cheese as a garnish

Preparation

Cut the tortillas into ¾-inch-wide (2-cm) strips; cut the strips in half. Coat a large nonstick frying pan with cooking spray. Add 2 teaspoons of oil and heat over medium-high heat. Add half of the tortilla pieces to the pan and stir-fry about 10 minutes until all the oil and cooking spray are absorbed and a few tortilla pieces are crisp. Remove the pieces and set aside. Add cooking spray and 2 more teaspoons oil to the pan and fry the remaining tortilla pieces.

Put the garlic, tomatoes, chiles, and salt in a blender and blend until nearly smooth. Heat 1 teaspoon of oil in a nonstick frying pan over medium-high heat. Add the contents of the blender, and cook for 3 minutes, stirring occasionally. Add the *epazote*, stir, and cook for 2 minutes.

Add the tortilla pieces to the sauce, and mix. Reduce the heat to medium-low and cook for 1–2 minutes until most of the sauce is absorbed. Divide into individual portions, sprinkle with cheese, and serve.

Variations

Chilaquiles Verdes con Pollo: Use *Salsa Verde Cocida* (page 51) in place of tomato sauce (be sure to still add *epazote*) and top individual servings with shredded chicken (two split breasts) and nonfat sour cream thinned with skim milk.

Nutrition Information
Amounts per Serving

Calories: 391
Calories from fat: 21.5%
Total fat: 9.8 g
Saturated fat: 1.6 g

Cholesterol: 2 mg
Carbohydrates: 70.2 g
Protein: 10.5 g
Sodium: 528 mg

✒ Salsa de Huevo
Scrambled Eggs in Roasted Tomato and Chile Sauce

Yield: 4 servings

Spanish speakers may wonder what's up with the name of this recipe, which translates inaccurately as "egg sauce." Although I could not discover the origin of the misleading moniker, I did find this scrumptious breakfast to be one of the finest of the Veracruz-Oaxaca region.

Ingredients

3 large ripe tomatoes
1–4 *chiles jalapeños*
½ teaspoon salt
2 teaspoons olive oil
1 slice white onion, ¼-inch thick (0.5-cm)
¼ cup (60 ml) chopped cilantro, loosely packed, or *epazote*
2 eggs
1½ cups (375 ml) egg substitute
8 corn tortillas

Preparation

Broil and peel tomatoes and chiles as described on pages 18–19. Remove the chile stems, chop the chiles, and put them in a blender. Seed and roughly chop two tomatoes and add them to the blender. Chop the third tomato and add it, with its juices, to the blender. Add the salt and pulse-blend contents to a chunky sauce; do not purée.

Put the oil and onion in an aluminum frying pan and heat over medium-high heat. Blacken the onion, then discard. Add the contents of the blender to the pan, stirring immediately to minimize spattering. Simmer for 8–10 minutes until the sauce has thickened slightly. Stir in the cilantro or *epazote*, then remove from the heat.

Beat the eggs in a bowl. Add the egg substitute and beat to blend. Coat a large nonstick frying pan or sauté pan with cooking spray and heat over medium heat. Add the egg mixture and allow it to set as for an omelet. Cut the omelet into 4 to 6 large pieces, flip, and cook until done. Add the sauce, mix, and heat for 2 minutes. Serve with warm tortillas.

Nutrition Information
Amounts per Serving

Calories: 269

Calories from fat: 24.1%

Total fat: 7.3 g

Saturated fat: 1.4 g

Cholesterol: 106 mg

Carbohydrates: 34.9 g

Protein: 17.1 g

Sodium: 680 mg

∾ Huevos Motuleños
Tortillas Topped with Black Beans, Eggs, and Peas

Yield: 4 servings

This is Yucatán's version of *Huevos Rancheros*. Turkey ham makes a wonderful substitute for the pork version normally used. Serve with *Arroz a la Mexicana* (page 137) on the side and *Jalapeños en Escabeche* (pages 81–82) as a relish.

Ingredients

1 ½ cups (375 ml) *Frijoles Negros de Olla* (pages 132–133) or 1 can black beans, 15 oz (420 g)
Salsa Ranchera (page 52)
4 corn tortillas, 5 inches (12.5 cm) in diameter
4 large eggs
Salt, to taste
¾ cup (185 ml) frozen peas, thawed
¼ pound (100 g) diced or chopped turkey ham

Preparation

Preheat oven to 375°F (190°C). Warm the beans in a medium saucepan. Warm *Salsa Ranchera* in a separate saucepan. Place the tortillas on a cookie sheet and bake for 3–5 minutes or until warm. Remove and place one tortilla on a plate; wrap the others in a dry dishtowel.

Coat a nonstick frying pan with plenty of cooking spray and heat over medium heat. Fry one egg sunny-side up and sprinkle with salt. Cover the tortilla with plenty of black beans, then top with egg. Cover the egg with *Salsa Ranchera* and top with a couple tablespoons each of peas and turkey ham. Repeat this process for the remaining three servings. Serve.

Variations

For a Caribbean touch, add a few slices of banana as the final topper.

Nutrition Information
Amounts per Serving

Calories: 382	Cholesterol: 228 mg
Calories from fat: 20.9%	Carbohydrates: 52.7 g
Total fat: 9.1 g	Protein: 24.9 g
Saturated fat: 2.5 g	Sodium: 1,064 mg

∾ Ensalada Tropical Especial
Tropical Fruit Salad with Yogurt and Honey

Yield: 6 servings

This fresh fruit salad is a hit with tourists and Mexicans alike.

Ingredients

½ small pineapple, peeled and cored
½ extremely ripe small Mexican red (*mirasol*) papaya or 1 Hawaiian
   papaya, peeled and seeded
½ small cantaloupe, peeled and seeded
¼ watermelon, seeded
2 large bananas
2 cups (500 ml) nonfat plain yogurt thinned with ½ cup (125 ml)
   skim milk
Honey as a garnish
Wheat germ or low-fat granola as a garnish

Preparation

Cut the pineapple, papaya, cantaloupe, and watermelon into bite-size pieces.
Peel and slice the bananas. Fill plates with equal portions of each fruit.
Pour the yogurt over the fruit on each plate. Drizzle a bit of honey over the
fruit and top with wheat germ or granola. Serve.

Nutrition Information
Amounts per Serving

Calories: 389	Cholesterol: 1 mg
Calories from fat: 6.1%	Carbohydrates: 90.9 g
Total fat: 2.9 g	Protein: 8.5 g
Saturated fat: 0.2 g	Sodium: 74 mg

∾ Sopes
Corn Tortilla Pies with Salsa

Yield: 6 servings

Although this recipe is a bit involved, the time spent preparing these favorite Mexican snacks is worth the trouble. Or, as a *Mexicano* might say, ¡*Vale la pena!*

Tortilla Ingredients
3 cups (750 ml) or 1 pound (1½ kg) corn flour (*masa harina*)
2 cups (500 ml) water

Filling Ingredients
2 large split chicken breasts
Salsa Ranchera (page 52) and *Salsa Verde Cocida* (page 51)
1½ cups (375 ml) *Frijoles Negros de Olla* (pages 132–133) or 1 can black beans, 15 oz (420 g)
¼ pound (100 g) crumbled *queso ranchero* or grated parmesan cheese
½ cup (125 ml) nonfat sour cream thinned with 2 tablespoons skim milk
2–4 *chiles serranos*, finely chopped, as a garnish
Chopped cilantro as a garnish
1 medium white onion, finely chopped, as a garnish

Preparation
Poach and shred the chicken breast as described on page 19. Mix the flour and water as described under "Preparing *Masa*" (page 91). Pinch enough *masa* to form a ball 1½ inches (3.75 cm) in diameter. Proceed as described under "Pressing *Masa*" (page 91), but press the tortilla to only about 4 inches (10 cm) in diameter, leaving it slightly thicker than as for a regular tortilla. Remove the plastic/tortilla/plastic "sandwich" from the press.

Heat a nonstick frying pan over medium-high heat for 5 minutes or until it's reached a constant temperature. Peel the plastic from the tortilla. Lay the tortilla in the pan and heat until facedown side is lightly speckled with brown spots. Flip the tortilla and pinch up its sides into a lip while it is cooking, forming a miniature pie-like shell. Heat until the dough is cooked all the way through, remove, and store wrapped in a dry dishtowel. Repeat this process until all the masa is used.

Warm the *Salsa Ranchera*, *Salsa Verde Cocida*, and beans in separate saucepans. Coat a large nonstick frying pan with cooking spray and heat over medium heat. Add two or three tortilla shells and heat for 45–60 seconds until warmed through. Remove and fill with *Salsa Ranchera*, black beans, and cheese, or with *Salsa Verde*, chicken, and thinned sour cream. Repeat process until all tortilla shells are used. Top with chiles, onion, and cilantro, and serve.

Nutrition Information
Amounts per Serving

Calories: 490　　　　　　Cholesterol: 33 mg
Calories from fat: 12.6%　Carbohydrates: 83.4 g
Total fat: 7.1 g　　　　　Protein: 28.2 g
Saturated fat: 1.8 g　　　Sodium: 709 mg

ᵔ *Huevos Envueltos*
Eggs Wrapped in Tortillas with Tomatillo Sauce

Yield: 3 servings

The mixture of sour cream and *Salsa Verde Cocida*—a Mexican favorite—is highlighted in this dish from the west coast state of Jalisco, the birthplace of mariachi music.

Ingredients
½ cup (125 ml) nonfat sour cream
¼ cup (60 ml) evaporated skim milk
2 teaspoons corn oil
½ small white onion
1–2 *chiles serranos*
1 cup (250 ml) egg substitute
Salt, to taste
6 corn tortillas, 5 inches (12.5 cm) in diameter
Salsa Verde Cocida (page 51)
½ cup (125 ml) shredded reduced-fat mozzarella cheese
Chopped cilantro as a garnish

Preparation
Preheat oven to 375°F (190°C). Mix the sour cream and skim milk in a bowl and set aside. Heat the oil in a nonstick frying pan over medium heat. Add the onion and chiles and sauté for 3–5 minutes until the onion is soft but not brown. Pour the egg substitute into a pan, stir, and allow to set. Flip, season with salt, and cook until done. Cover the pan and remove from the heat.

Warm the tortillas as for rolling enchiladas (page 49). Place equal portions of eggs in each and fold over. Place egg-filled tortillas in a baking dish, overlapping them slightly so that they remain folded. Bake for 10 minutes. Warm the *Salsa Verde* in a saucepan. Remove the tortillas, cover with salsa, and top with cream mixture and cheese. Place under the broiler until the cheese is melted and just starting to brown. Remove, top with cilantro, and serve.

Nutrition Information
Amounts per Serving

Calories: 321   Cholesterol: 16 mg
Calories from fat: 28.1% Carbohydrates: 36.8 g
Total fat: 10.2 g   Protein: 21.8 g
Saturated fat: 1.8 g   Sodium: 561 mg

Chapter 10

Bebidas/Beverages

Although you cannot drink the water south of the border, Mexico offers many outstanding and safe alternatives to the tourist stand-bys of *refrescos* (soda) and *cervezas* (beer).

Ingredients such as fruit, rice, and flowers are combined with purified water to create an assortment of thirst-quenching soft drinks appealing to the eye as well as the taste buds. Served from minia-ture plastic barrels throughout the country's streets and markets, these colorful refreshments are the perfect recourse on days when there seems to be no escape from the heat. On the other hand, when the temperature drops below freezing high in the villages of the Sierra Madres, locals warm themselves with mugs of special brews made of corn, coffee, or chocolate—staples in Mexico since antiq-uity.

Hot or cold—and never too hot or too cold, for Mexicans be-lieve this is a sure way of getting sick—*las bebidas Mexicanas* are sure to please.

∾ *Naranjada*
Orange Soft Drink

Yield: 2 quarts (2 liters)

In Mexico, oranges tend to have green, tough skins that make them difficult to peel. Thus, they are seldom eaten as a snack, passing instead straight to the juicer to be served as fresh orange juice or as this all-natural orange-ade.

Ingredients

2½ cups (625 ml) freshly squeezed orange juice (about 10 oranges)
5½ cups (1375 ml) water
⅔ cup (160 ml) sugar

Preparation

Put orange juice in a 2-quart (2-liter) container. Add water and sugar and stir to dissolve. Serve in tall glasses over ice.

Nutrition Information
Serving: 1 cup (250 ml)
Amounts per Serving

Calories: 99
Calories from fat: 1.4%
Total fat: 0.2 g
Saturated fat: 0 g

Cholesterol: 0 mg
Carbohydrates: 24.7 g
Protein: 0.5 g
Sodium: 6 mg

∾ *Aguas Frescas de Frutas*
Fresh Fruit Soft Drink

Yield: 3 servings

Mexico boasts an impressive assortment of fruits, most available year-round at low prices. Every town has at least one fruit bar, where people convene to socialize over fresh fruit salads, frozen fruit bars, and especially these ubiquitous fruit drinks.

Ingredients

3 cups (750 ml) chopped cantaloupe, pineapple, guava, pear, or
    seeded watermelon
2 cups (500 ml) water
3 tablespoons sugar

Preparation

Put fruit in a blender. Add water and sugar and blend on a low speed for about 15 seconds; do not make the juice too frothy. Strain into a pitcher and set aside for 10 minutes to allow air bubbles to settle. Serve in tall glasses over ice.

Nutrition Information: Cantaloupe Drink
Serving: 1 cup (250 ml)
Amounts per Serving

Calories: 104
Calories from fat: 3.6%
Total fat: 0.4 g
Saturated fat: 0 g

Cholesterol: 0 mg
Carbohydrates: 25.9 g
Protein: 1.4 g
Sodium: 19 mg

∾ *Licuados*
Fresh Fruit Milk Shake

Yield: About 1 quart (1 liter)

You can identify a juice bar in Mexico by the oranges, papayas, bananas, and mangos on display and the pictures of tropical fruits painted on the walls. Stopping in for a cold *Licuado* or *Agua Fresca*, prepared with purified ice or water, is a nice respite from the scorching heat.

Ingredients

5 ice cubes
2 cups (500 ml) chopped ripe strawberries, banana, papaya, or
     peach, or 1 ½ cups (375 ml) mango
2 cups (500 ml) skim milk
3 tablespoons sugar

Preparation

Put ice cubes, fruit, milk, and sugar in a blender, and blend for 20–30 seconds until smooth and frothy. Serve in individual glasses.

∾ Tips

Use 1 cup (250 ml) skim milk and 1 cup (250 ml) evaporated skim milk for a creamier shake.

Nutrition Information: Strawberry Shake
Serving: 1 cup (250 ml)
Amounts per Serving

Calories: 101	Cholesterol: 2 mg
Calories from fat: 4.2%	Carbohydrates: 20.5 g
Total fat: 0.5 g	Protein: 4.6 g
Saturated fat: 0.2 g	Sodium: 6.4 mg

✎ *Agua de Jamaica*
Hibiscus Soft Drink

Yield: 1 gallon (4 liters)

Agua de Jamaica is one of the most popular soft drinks in Mexico. Known for its fruity flavor and dark red color, the caffeine-free punch makes a wonderful alternative to soda, iced tea, or powdered drinks.

Ingredients

3 cups (750 ml) dried hibiscus flowers, loosely packed, or 8 hibiscus tea bags
1 gallon (4 liters) water
2 cups (500 ml) sugar

Preparation

Boil the flowers or tea bags in a gallon of water about 20 minutes until the liquid is dark red. Allow it to cool. Strain, add sugar, and stir to dissolve. Cool in the refrigerator for 30 minutes, then serve in tall glasses over ice.

Variations

Agua de Jamaica del Sol: Fill a sun-tea container with a gallon of water, add flowers or tea bags, screw on the cap, and set in the sun for 5 hours. Strain the liquid, add sugar, and stir to dissolve. Cool in the refrigerator for 30 minutes, then serve in tall glasses over ice.

Nutrition Information
Serving: 1 cup (250 ml)
Amounts per serving

Calories: 103	Cholesterol: 0
Calories from fat: 0	Carbohydrates: 25 g
Total fat: 0	Protein: 0
Saturated fat: 0	Sodium: 7 mg

❧ *Café de Olla*/Spiced Coffee

Yield: 2 quarts (2 liters)

Although their country produces fine coffee beans, Mexicans actually prefer to drink instant coffee. Most restaurants, in fact, merely serve hot water to mix with the granules set out on the tables. Fortunately for gringos, a cup of "pot coffee," as the name of this recipe translates, can occasionally be scared up.

Ingredients

2 quarts (2 liters) water
2 cinnamon sticks, 6-inches long (15-cm) each
⅓ rounded cup (80 ml) brown sugar
2 whole cloves (optional)
¾ cup (185 ml) ground dark-roast coffee

Preparation

Put the water in a large pot. Add the cinnamon sticks, sugar, and cloves. Stir to dissolve the sugar, and bring to a boil. Boil vigorously for 15 minutes. Remove from the heat, add coffee, and stir well; cover and steep for 5 minutes. Strain the coffee into another pot or thermal carafe, then serve in individual mugs.

❧ Tips

Use ½ cup (125 ml) brown sugar for a sweeter cup o' joe.

Nutrition Information
Serving: 1 cup (250 ml)
Amounts per Serving

Calories: 28	Cholesterol: 0 mg
Calories from fat: 1.6%	Carbohydrates: 7.3 g
Total fat: 0.1 g	Protein: 0.1 g
Saturated fat: 0 g	Sodium: 10 mg

∿ *Café con Leche*/Spiced Coffee with Warmed Milk

Yield: 2 quarts (2 liters)

I'm always tempted to call this beverage "*Leche con Café*," since it contains such a large quantity of milk. By any name, this rich brew is a Mexican favorite, especially when made with instant coffee (recipe follows) and served for breakfast with sugared bread, or *pan dulce*.

Ingredients

1 quart (1 liter) *Café de Olla* (page 212)
1 quart (1 liter) evaporated skim milk

Preparation

Bring the coffee to a boil in a saucepan. Meanwhile, warm the milk in a separate saucepan to just below a boil. Remove the coffee from the heat and let cool for 30 seconds. Serve in individual mugs, filling each half with coffee and half with hot milk.

Variations

Mexicans tend to prefer instant coffee, resulting in this speedy version of *Café con Leche*: Use 1 teaspoon instant coffee per mug. Heat 2 quarts (2 liters) evaporated skim milk, as above. Fill mugs with milk, and stir. Top with a pinch of ground cinnamon, and serve.

Nutrition Information
Serving: 1 cup (250 ml)
Amounts per Serving

Calories: 57	Cholesterol: 2 mg
Calories from fat: 3.9%	Carbohydrates: 9.6 g
Total fat: 0.2 g	Protein: 4.2 g
Saturated fat: 0.1 g	Sodium: 68 mg

❧ *Horchata de Arroz*/Rice Milk

Yield: 2 quarts (2 liters)

Technically, *Horchata* can also be made of coconut or melon seeds, but the rice variation seems to be the favorite. One special version I tasted in Oaxaca City was topped with edible flower petals and crumbled walnut.

Ingredients

2 quarts (2 liters) water
2 cups (500 ml) long-grain white rice
¾ cup (185 ml) sugar
¾ teaspoon cinnamon
1 cup (250 ml) evaporated skim milk
¼ teaspoon vanilla extract

Preparation

Bring the water to a boil in a large pot. Remove from the heat, add rice, and stir. Let the rice soak for 30 minutes, stirring occasionally. Stir in the sugar, cinnamon, skim milk, and vanilla. Transfer the contents of the pot to a blender and blend in two or three batches as needed. Strain each batch through cheesecloth or a fine strainer into a large pitcher. Stir well and serve in tall glasses over ice.

Nutrition Information
Serving: 1 cup (250 ml)
Amounts per Serving

Calories: 221
Calories from fat: 0.4%
Total fat: 0.1 g
Saturated fat: 0 g

Cholesterol: 1 mg
Carbohydrates: 52.6 g
Protein: 2.5 g
Sodium: 47 mg

∾ *Champurrado*
Chocolate Corn Drink

Yield: 6 servings

A standard holiday beverage in Mexico is *atole*, a warmed mixture of corn flour, cinnamon, and brown sugar. Combine this with another Mexican favorite, chocolate, and the result is this rich-and-creamy delight.

Ingredients

6 cups (1 ½ liters) water
¾ cup (375 ml) corn flour (*masa harina*)
¼ cup (60 ml) brown sugar
3 tablets, 2 oz (56 g) each, Mexican chocolate
1 teaspoon of cinnamon

Preparation

Put 3 cups (750 ml) water in a blender. Add the corn flour, sugar, chocolate, and cinnamon; and purée. Transfer the purée to a large saucepan, add the remaining 3 cups (750 ml) water, and heat for 20 minutes over low heat, stirring constantly, until thick and creamy. Serve hot in individual mugs.

∾ Tips

Add more milk for a creamier *Champurrado*. Use more water for a thinner version.

Nutrition Information
Serving: 1 cup (250 ml)
Amounts per Serving

Calories: 175	Cholesterol: 1 mg
Calories from fat: 14.1%	Carbohydrates: 34.4 g
Total fat: 2.8 g	Protein: 3.6 g
Saturated fat: 0.5 g	Sodium: 35 mg

International Measurements Conversion Chart

The following conversions have been rounded off to reflect normal measurment uses in different parts of the world. Please note that using these conversions may subtly alter your recipe results.

Spoon Measurement Conversions

American	Metric
¼ teaspoon	1 ml
½ teaspoon	2 ml
1 teaspoon	5 ml

Liquid Measurement Conversions

American	Metric	Imperial	Australian
1 tablespoon (½ oz)	15 ml	½ fl oz	½ tablespoon
2 tablespoons (1 oz)	30 ml	1 fl oz	1 tablespoon
¼ cup (2 oz)	60 ml	2 fl oz	2 tablespoons
⅓ cup (3 oz)	80 ml	3 fl oz	¼ cup
½ cup (4 oz)	125 ml	4 fl oz	⅓ cup
⅔ cup (5 oz)	160 ml	5 fl oz	½ cup
¾ cup (6 oz)	185 ml	6 fl oz	⅔ cup
1 cup (8 oz)	250 ml	8 fl oz	¾ cup

American Measurement Equivalents

3 teaspoons = 1 tablespoon

4 tablespoons = ¼ cup

½ cup = 4 fl oz

2 cups = 1 pint

1 pint = 16 fl oz

2 pints = 1 quart

Weights

American/UK	Metric
1 oz	30 g
2 oz	60 g
4 oz (¼ pound)	125 g
5 oz (⅓ pound)	155 g
6 oz	185 g
7 oz	220 g
8 oz (½ pound)	250 g
9 oz	280 g
10 oz	315 g
12 oz (¾ pound)	375 g
16 oz (1 pound)	500 g (½ kg)
1½ pounds	¾ kg
2 pounds	1 kg
3 pounds	1½ kg
4 pounds	2 kg
5 pounds	2¼ kg

Oven Temperatures

Fahrenheit	Celsius	Gas Marks
140°F	60°C	
160°F	70°C	
250°F	120°C	½
275°F	135°C	1
300°F	150°C	2
325°F	160°C	3
350°F	175°C	4
375°F	190°C	5
400°F	205°C	6
425°F	220°C	7
450°F	230°C	8

Index

Patrick Earvolino

Author Patrick Earvolino has experimented with and sampled numerous ethnic recipes in addition to TexMex and Mexican foods, including his family's Neapolitan fare, Cuban salsas, and Bangladeshi curries. Trained in chemistry at New York's prestigious Rensselaer Polytechnic Institute, Patrick's interest in Mexican cooking is "fueled by a desire to get closer to the ingredients responsible for my growing addiction" to hot and spicy food. This addiction is supplemented by his health-conscious mind, which guides him toward innovative and fascinating ways to prepare the dishes he loves while still respecting his body and the authenticity of the cuisine. He has traveled extensively around Mexico, where he also studied intensive Spanish and cooking. When not eating, Patrick composes songs and writes food articles and restaurant reviews for the *Austin Chronicle*. He works as a science editor for the Holt, Rinehart and Winston Company in Austin, Texas.

Photo copyright John Langford

Photo copyright David Omer

Lisa Kirkpatrick

Artist Lisa Kirkpatrick lives in Austin, Texas, with her husband and two cats. She has a B.F.A. from the University of Texas at Austin, and works as the promotion designer for *Texas Monthly* magazine. She enjoys traveling to Mexico to experience the culture and to add to her collection of Mexican folk art.